CREATIVE IDEAS FOR
ALTERNATIVE SACRAMENTAL WORSHIP

Creative Ideas for Alternative Sacramental Worship

Simon Rundell

CANTERBURY PRESS
Norwich

© Simon Rundell 2010

First published in 2010 by Canterbury Press
Editorial office
108–114 Golden Lane,
London EC1Y 0TG, UK

Second impression 2015

Canterbury Press is an imprint of Hymns Ancient & Modern Ltd
(a registered charity)
13A Hellesdon Park Road,
Norwich NR6 5DR

www.canterburypress.co.uk

British Library Cataloguing in Publication data

A catalogue record for this book is available
from the British Library

978 1 84825 023 9

Typeset by Regent Typesetting, London
Printed and bound by
CPI Group (UK) Ltd, Croydon, CR0 4YY

Contents

1

Preamble

I'm going to admit it first before you draw the same conclusion in about five pages: I'm no theologian. My calling is to *do* first and foremost and then reflect on it long afterwards – and reflect in some indefinable qualitative and decidedly unclinical, unhygienic and definitely non-theological way. My charism is concerned with evangelism, and even at theological college I knew that the ivory tower was never going to be my natural home.

So, if you're searching for a deep theological exploration of the sacramental life in current emerging churches, backed by heavy theological references and wide-ranging research, then I suspect you have stolen the wrong book: put it back now and no one will be any the wiser.

If, however, you have some sense that you are being drawn to a sacramental form of worship from either outside or within the Church, want to take it further and even out to the cutting edge of evangelism (for that is naturally where Jesus may be truly found) then you might have found the resource you are looking for.

You might think that this book is crammed with technological wizardry which will be beyond you, but be assured – this is not rocket science: it does not demand teenager-level techie skills, vast resources or masses of shiny electronics; this is more about the sacraments, those essential mysteries of God. I want to lay out what you *need* to know about sacramental alternative worship, so that by the end of this book you will be brimming with ideas, new skills and, I pray, the vision to do wonderfully creative things in sacramental worship.

Whether you are from a background that has had nothing to do with sacraments before, have shied away from all this high-church nonsense (or even in your previous church, regarded all this as idolatry) but are still searching, yearning for a more profound encounter with the living and present Jesus; or whether you are from an Anglo-Catholic, Roman or Orthodox background and want to give that which is already a major facet of your spiritual life a new and radical twist; I trust that the possibilities that are laid bare here might be of benefit to you all.

This is not an off-the-shelf collection of material for you to plug in. It is not 'Fresh Expression in a package' which enables you to tick the box and meet the parish's demand to do something, *anything*. Rather, it is a toolkit: a collection of resources and I hope an inspiration for new and original creativity in your worship.

To be a Christian is to be a theologian. To speak of God, to pray, to reflect on him is to act theologically. Theology worked out in practice is best seen in worship, the purpose of our very being, the natural response to God.

'Adopt, adapt and improve' was the motto of the Round Table, and it should be the theme of this book: take from this and add of your own. Fresh Expressions are a reflection of your own community, the charism of you and your people, and not just what I can offer you in this book.

Now, get out there and prepare to worship!

Simon+
Feast of the Nativity, 2009

1.1 Acknowledgements

There are influences and possibly sources that will probably go unacknowledged, to whom I apologise. However, respect, love and thanks are due to Jonathon Barnbrook for permission to use his artwork; Mark Steadman, Toby Wright, Ron Cole, Caroline Rhodes, Ruth Innes and Cheryl Lawrie for their liturgies, which have contributed so much to the *Blesséd* worship over the years; Emma Rundell and Vickie Williams for their photographs and the ministry of lugging; Liam Rundell for being the enabler of it all; Philip North, Wealands Bell and the Shrine of Our Lady of Walsingham for such inspiration and such laughter; to all who have travelled with *Blesséd* over the years, all the priests and youth ministers who have found us space and a few quid to do this stuff and dealt with the fallout afterwards – thank you for your prayers; and finally Lou for being the best mentor and soulmate ever.

1.2 Introduction

You might have thought that after 2,000 years we would have found a better way to encounter God. With all of our technology, communications expertise and simple experience, surely God can be found without all this messing around with old-fashioned mystery and symbols? Hasn't anyone got his email address yet?

And yet, the most fundamental expressions of the Christian faith lie in modern forms of that which is most ancient: broken bread and wine outpoured – signs and symbols which hint at the presence of God in our midst and point to his *otherness*.

If you went to Catechism or Confirmation preparation, you would be schooled in the definition of a sacrament as 'an outward visible sign of an inward spiritual grace',[1] meaning that any sacrament combines the physical and tangible of this world with something inward of God. Edward Schillebeeckx[2] concluded that the first 'primordial' sacrament was therefore Jesus Christ himself: both God and Man indivisible. It is not possible to separate the God from the human form of Jesus, and neither is it possible to separate the grace of God from any of the other sacraments. You cannot point at an atom inside a crumb of bread and declare 'There is God' because God is there throughout.

By this process, we should also conclude that the Church itself is a sacramental sign of God's grace. We should understand the Church to be not the building itself, nor any particular Church establishment (despite what some would infallibly claim as sole authority), but the gathering of people in community to worship God. The outward sign is the people, and in the inward grace is the manifestation of the Holy Spirit in the life and worship of the Church. *Ekklesia*[3] is a Greek word meaning 'community' and only latterly came to mean the Church itself. Any community gathered in worship is therefore Church, no matter how structured, formal or rag-bag it may appear.

This understanding of Christ and the Church as sacraments was influential upon the Vatican II Council, and changes the way in which we perceive the other seven sacraments as accepted by the Church. They become not mechanistic manifestations of the Church but, rather, dynamic and fluid revelations of God: mysteries which speak of God's love and grace when words run out. Speaking of Jesus, the end of the Gospel of John says:

---

1 J. H. Newman (1841), *Tract 90: Remarks on Certain Passages in the 39 Articles*, available online at: <http://anglicanhistory.org/tracts/tract90/section7.html>, accessed 4 April 2010.

2 E. Schillebeeckx (1963), *Christ the Sacrament of the Encounter with God*. Kansas City: Sheed, Andrews & McMeel.

3 *Ekklesia*: Strongs Number 1577. See <http://strongsnumbers.com/greek/1577.htm>, accessed 10 February 2010. This is the Greek word from which we get 'ecclesiastical'.

if every one of his words were written down, I suppose that the world itself
could not contain the books that would be written. (John 21.25)

Christ is THE Word,[4] and has not yet been fully expressed or enunciated in this
world, and today uses the Spirit, the Church and the sacraments to continue that
dialogue with creation.

The other seven sacraments accepted by the majority of the Church are based
upon scripture, tradition and the revelation of God through their very existence. To disregard some of these as 'not of scripture' is to place our God firmly
between the pages of a book, rather than see scripture as one of God's revelations, and perhaps even a sacrament in itself. We should be wary of making our
God too small.

These sacraments are:

First, the two sacraments explicitly documented in scripture:

• Baptism, initiation into faith.
• The Eucharist, the key sacrament of the Church, commonly called the Mass.

Followed by those whose presence in scripture is either implicit, or which have
been sanctified by the tradition of the Church[5]

• Confirmation, adult commitment to faith.
• Marriage, the calling of two individuals to each other in the eyes of God.
• Ordination, or the setting apart of individuals for ministry.
• Reconciliation with God, the end result of confession.
• Healing, culminating in a good death.

When communities start to explore the sacramental life, they focus principally
upon the first two: Baptism and the Mass, which initiates and sustains the people
of God. Naturally, this book is primarily concerned with Eucharistic worship,
but we should be wary of narrowing ourselves to these scriptural sacraments. It
is true that Confirmation, Marriage and Ordination demand ecclesial structures
and order, but any ecclesial community, no matter how worldwide or how local,
should be working to initiate, sustain, commit, heal and reconcile at the very
least, with Marriage and Ordination quickly developing out of the others as God
leads them.

---

4 John 1.1.
5 Which of course amounts to the same thing: holy scripture is a product of the Church
(inspired by the Holy Spirit), not the other way round.

I want to go further than these formal sacramental definitions. *Blesséd* (see Chapter 2) does not just see God limited to a community, a building, a piece of bread, a drop of wine or one individual. The fingerprints of God can be seen throughout the world, and so *Blesséd* declares all of life to be sacramental. When this is explored to its extreme, there becomes nothing profane, nothing irreligious, nothing which is beyond the power or scope of God's love or forgiveness.

1.3 Fresh Expressions?

Many will read this book desperate to create a Fresh Expression. Fresh Expressions is a beast quite unclear in the minds of many: an umbrella of disparate groups, thinkers, communities and ideas that cross denominational boundaries and traditions. It can be a travelling circus of good ideas or it can be some kind of corporate juggernaut set up to disturb the gentle calm of Choral Evensong. Many of the communities known as a part of the Fresh Expressions bandwagon existed long before there was a budget in the Church for it, and I am convinced will exist long after the nametags have run out.

There seems to be a subtext developing in the Church which says that every self-respecting parish should have a health & safety officer[6] and a Fresh Expression (although not necessarily in that order), and so the scramble begins. I am reminded of the rush by the record companies to sign punk bands after the Sex Pistols, and girl/boy bands after the Spice Girls: it doesn't matter, it must just be *fresh*. And so the scramble to do something begins. It might even be why you bought this book.

I'm going to state the obvious: Rome was not Corinth, was not Antioch and certainly was not Jerusalem. The Gospels (and their intended audiences) and the writings of the New Testament canon attest to different needs, different methods, different starting places and different ears. An evangelism course written for a well-off west London congregation doesn't quite hit the spot in considerably poorer urban Portsmouth.[7] One fresh expression which grows out of York nightclubs is by necessity different from one which started with teenagers on the south coast: different needs, different aims, different techniques.

What the Fresh Expressions movement has always tried to say is that it should be 'do-it-yourself', but the scramble to copy the most innovative ideas and implement them without inculturation into the local context results in churches that

---

6 Important, but secondary to the mission of the Church.

7 Please feel free to make up your own comparisons based on your own context.

look remarkably like High Streets up and down the country: bland, homogenized and ultimately not at all fresh.

Yes, *Messy Church* is brilliant, but what can you innovate in your locality that is as original? Yes, a gathering in a café with a DJ is a cool idea, but not if it becomes the Starbucks of church outreach itself: it is replicated everywhere when what we really want (to see this café metaphor to its conclusion) is a local independent coffee shop which serves its own tasty roast in its own quirky surroundings.

Where I think Fresh Expressions is at its most effective is when it allows disparate communities to seek their own charism within a caring and supportive umbrella: the established Church has clear lines of accountability to prevent abuse and demagoguery, a theology that can be used as a framework to explore faith, and sometimes kick against it, and an institution that can ultimately bankroll these fledgling forms of mission by providing space, expenses, advertising and a shell from which these emerging communities may arise. Some might argue that a Fresh Expression does not meet the definition of Emerging Church because it is linked so closely to the Establishment, but I must argue that all the really transformative innovations in theology, ecclesiology and worship, from the rise of evangelicalism to the Oxford Movement, happen within an established ecclesial structure.

As these Fresh Expressions mature and develop, many find that their community is incomplete without the sacraments.

So, after all that, does what is produced enable us to tick the box marked 'Fresh Expression'? I am not so sure, because so much has been given to its corporate branding that I, and, I am sure, many of you, now view it with little more than cynicism. However:

- I would want to argue that if anything we are doing is stale, tired, weather-beaten and not really very dearly loved, then it is a waste of time, effort and mission.
- If anything we do does not stimulate the heart and soul for Christ, then it must be ditched.
- If anything that takes place in church does not stretch and challenge the faith, then it is not gospel-shaped and has no place in church.
- If each and every Mass that your clergy says is not a Fresh Expression of faith, then I would want to challenge them to go back to the ordinal and be reminded of the ordination charge.

1.4 About this Book

Many books in this *Creatve Ideas* series dive straight in with a myriad of examples, but my philosophy is that the bulk of creative and innovative worship should come from you: your local community and the skills among you. This is why *Blesséd* looks like it does, and why your liturgy should reflect YOU.

Chapter 2 tells the story of *Blesséd* and some of its philosophy of mission and liturgy.

Chapter 3 is filled with good advice and insight into the tools of this work: how to get the stuff out of your heads and onto the hard disk, and thence into the sacred space.

Chapter 4 is filled with our good ideas for you to use, adapt and improve in your worship. This includes items for use in the Eucharist, Labyrinths and other multimedia installations, and other meditations and useful liturgy elements, including one or two complete liturgies. It is deliberately incomplete so you can make something of your own.

2

Sacrament as Mission: The Experience of *Blesséd*

My problem is that I've never been conventional: always been in trouble, always been at the back of class irritating the authorities who tell us how it should be done, and why it has to be like it is.

Blesséd[1] is, I suppose, a reflection of this: a loose collection of individuals and their charisms that almost on purpose seeks to take what we know and love and do it differently.

Blesséd gathers a dozen times a year in worship, almost always sacramental worship and usually as Mass, shaped by the liturgical seasons; and is continuing to seek (rather haphazardly) to become a more distinct non-parochial, non-geographical ecclesial community as it tries to support itself through social networking and other media between gatherings for worship.

On one level, *Blesséd* is solidly traditional – deeply sacramental, unashamedly Anglo-Catholic, soaked in gin and the cycle of the daily office; and on another it seeks to blow that world apart – to declare the whole of creation as sacramental, and our approach to God as immersive, multisensory and wildly, rabidly inclusive.

Blesséd sees itself as steeped in values which have been passed down to us from the apostles and the saints, moulded by Holy Mother Church and shaped by the weight of theological consideration, liturgical practice and the pastoral needs of

---

1 <www.blessed.org.uk>.

the pilgrim people of God: a true manifestation of the spirit of Anglicanism if not its nature, which is frankly confused and even slightly offended by such an odd beast as *Blessèd*.

This chapter seeks to build on this curiously Anglican heritage: a catholic yet reformed heritage, to re-emphasize our mission and the proclamation of the gospel, and for us to be reminded that we already have the principal tool of mission to hand: the Mass.

One of the legacies of the Reformation was the rejection of the sensual and the sensuous. Our engagement with God is much more than simply what we say aloud, or even what we hear, but in sight (spectacle and ritual), smell, taste and touch we are enabled to engage both our minds and hearts in worship: we are creatures created to worship, but I suspect that the evangelical narrowness of *sola scriptura* cuts out many of our worshiping experiences by restricting our means of engaging with God. God is bigger than that.

Catholicism is a fundamental way of looking at the incarnation and the world as affected by the incarnation, and therefore our sacramental life is crucial, central even to the work of mission. Being authentically Catholic means being multisensory and opening ourselves to the outrageous and audacious possibilities which the incarnation offers to us.

Bishop Lindsay Urwin, in an article on the sacramental ministry in fresh mission, suggests that:

> One might argue that in a culture saturated with trivial, unmemorable and unreliable words, Christ-filled symbol and action might have more chance of breaking through [and being heard].[2]

When words run out, and they always run out when we are in an encounter with the indescribable, we turn to symbol and sign. Society is surrounded by symbol and sign, not to control us, but to enable us to engage with that which is beyond our experience: from the burning bush to the body and blood, our encounter with the sacred cannot solely be through word alone, for the soul encounters God on many levels.

Fundamentally, I believe that our primary encounter with God in worship is not an intellectual one, but an emotive one. Worship is one of the first ways in which seekers of faith encounter Christ, and when asked about their first dip in the worship ocean, they do not reflect on worship in terms of reason or logic, whether they were convinced by the argument, but how it made them feel.

---

2 S. Croft (2008), *Mission-Shaped Questions*. London: Church House Publishing, p. 31.

The experience of *Blesséd* shows how it is worship, and fundamentally sacramental worship, that is a key tool in breaking through the mundanity of every-
day life. In urban Portsmouth, we stepped out in mission to an extremely mixed
group of teenagers. Not having any money, resources or (quite frankly) any clue,
my first solution was simply to introduce a group of largely unchurched young
people in an open youth club to the church: the Lady Chapel in particular. In
the dark (lit only by candles and swathed in incense, around a cross, or an ikon,
projecting some words on a blank wall or the altar frontal), something wonderful happened: these young people who only months before were vying to knock
out as many quarterlight windows as they could, were able to grasp the presence
of God in their midst. Truly effective mission allows people to encounter God,
and the missioner simply turns up for the ride.

The last great swell of Anglo-Catholic mission in the UK was in the 1920s
and the 1930s and took place in poor, working-class slums where the beauty
and transcendence of worship lifted the people of God. It was through the sacraments that encounter took place. When we started to plan worship, a number of
our young people said independently, 'Well, it has to be a Mass doesn't it?', 'We
wanna do that fing with the bread and the wine, Farv.'[3] It is intriguing that they
sought to define themselves in terms of their relationship to the sacrament and

---

3 Actual quote: that's how some of us talk in Portsmouth.

yet not to be constrained by the traditions of it. For them, each element of the Mass was seen as being up for grabs, for a radical interpretation and a retelling of the story.

So, in 2002 (long before the 'Fresh Expressions' label was applied to everything outside of Choral Evensong), *Blesséd* was born – proclaiming Eucharist with funky backbeats, *Gloria* with dancing, sacrament with attitude. *Blesséd* sought to explore its sacramental heritage while proclaiming its ancient truths in new and creative ways. This has meant taking what we know and love, and asking how its story may be told for new generations.

For our community, the sacraments are the fount of all being: all life is sacramental and the sacramental life is the mechanism through which Almighty God and his creation encounter each other.

Blesséd seeks to encourage creativity first and foremost: the *Gloria* is tap-danced. Bread is kneaded. New prefaces are said and wine is consecrated by the bottle-load in unspoken action. Blessings are scribbled on a rocket and exploded in the night sky over Gosport. These creative, expressive ways are as real to these missional communities as were the first Eucharistic prayers of Hypolytus.

I am not advocating the throwing away of our carefully honed heritage in favour of some spiritual supermarket of technical wizardry and gimmicky Mass, but rather a creative and free-flowing use of the entire tradition of the Church: tradition which is not static, but dynamic and as engaging as the incarnation. To the other extreme, this creative flow should not be restricted to just 'youth services' or 'children's services', but as we find at St Thomas the Apostle, Elson,[4]

the parish that hosts *Blesséd*, creativity starts to infuse and cross-fertilize – we must be one of the few Anglo-Catholic parishes to use a projector at each Parish Mass – and we benefit from the flexibility and cost-effectiveness of projecting the entire liturgy and hymnody on screen each and every week.

One of the things I repeatedly hear after *Blesséd* worship, especially from fellow clergy, is 'Oh, I couldn't do anything like that – I am so untechnical', as if I am the holder of esoteric secrets.

But I am convinced that the best multisensory worship does not have to plug into the mains, and our key tools – incense, stones, flowing water, bread and wine transformed into the body and

---

4 <Visit www.saintthomaselson.org.uk>.

blood of Christ – are the best tools, and dancing pixels are there to support them. In the Victoria and Albert Museum is this work by Jonathon Barnbrook.[5]

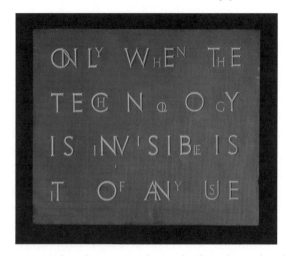

We should be constantly asking ourselves whether the technology we are using is appropriate or indeed is of any use. Ironically, this means any technology: how many people have been forced to wince through the murder of 'Shine Jesus Shine' played inappropriately on the organ, a full traditional choir butchering Taizé and a badly set up projector emasculating a worship chorus. The use of a microphone, a guitar, a video can enhance worship, but it can also be used to destroy that delicate moment where God and people come together.

We have to recognize that, while created in God's image, we are all different and have different learning styles and different approaches to God. Eneagram[6] and the Myers-Briggs Type Indicator[7] have backed this up – what works for me will not necessarily work for you.

Our problem has been that Archbishop Cranmer was clearly an auditory learner and our legacy as Anglicans is to be rigidly tied to the Prayer Book, the *Common Worship* text, to the hymnal and to the written word. Not all of us are like this. Some are – good for them. I (as you might have guessed) am not. I work best with visual stimulation backed up by the auditory; others love ritual and body prayer and have what educationalists refer to as a kinaesthetic bent. None of this is wrong. I used to think I was a terrible Christian because I was useless

---

5 Image used with permission of the artist. See <www.barnbrook.net> or Barnbrook Bible (2009)

6 D. R. Riso and R. Hudson (eds) (1997), *Personality Types*. Boston, MA: Houghton Mifflin.

7 Isabel Briggs with Peter B. Myers (1980, 1995), *Gifts Differing: Understanding Personality Type*. Mountain View, California: Davies-Black Publishing.

at silence: I'd get twitchy before the Blessed Sacrament until I did Myers-Briggs,[8] and the wise monk who analysed me said, 'You need something to do in prayer,' and gave me a rosary. My prayer life was transformed.

The Mass is, let's face it, the freshest of fresh expressions. As Pete Ward discussed in his book *Mass Culture*,[9] the Mass is an evangelistic opportunity and a missionary tool. It provides a unique opportunity for expressing the salvation story and the joy of the resurrection in word, song, action and ritual.

The Mass provides both fixed points of reference and an ever-changing cycle of encounter with God, and this mix of the familiar and the challenging provides a framework on which to hang new explorations of worship; rather than being a limit to fresh expressions of worship, it forms a skeleton upon which a new creation is formed. No community that seeks to be Christian can be said to be authentically so unless it gathers to break bread and pour wine and see that Christ is in its midst.

The Catholic spirituality might layer more over that and read much more (quite rightly) into that, but essentially, regardless of what it calls this engagement with Christ, regardless of its explicit sacramental theology, one thing all actually agree on is that Christ in some way is here among us.

---

8 Ibid.
9 P. Ward (1999), *Mass Culture*. Oxford: Bible Reading Fellowship.

The tools of mission are in the very hands of the priest, and excellent, creative, pre-thought-out and, above all, *well-performed liturgy* is supremely missional. All this messing around with pixels is only an extension of the central act of worship which it supports: the breaking of bread and the proclamation of the resurrection.

So often the sacramentally focused are prepared to beat themselves up about mission and their lack of activity in this area. But to them I say, the tools of mission are in your very hands – broken bread and wine outpoured are far more effective tools than an expensive missionary course purchased off the shelf at a conference. The 'Fan-the-Flame' missions are eucharistically centred for a reason, and the message of freedom, challenge and radical hospitality of the altar has so much to say to a society which is broken and confused by messages that say little to their context.

The Mass cannot be simply set down in a place and expected to do the work itself. The concept of priest as conduit of that sacrament has much to say about how we bring about that sacred encounter. Getting bodies through the door is not the end result but the beginning, and the sacramental encounter is the source of transformation and the cradle of faith.

Blesséd continues to push boundaries, set fire to carpets[10] and explore the sacramental life. Just as God has no boundaries, we do not know where this will lead our frail, fledgling community, but we are prepared to go along for the ride.

---

10 I am beginning to wonder if I will ever stop apologizing to Fr Draper and the Parish of St Mary the Virgin, Rowner. The lesson to be learnt is this: when you burn palm crosses with confessions written on them, make sure the bowls have a brick or a tile underneath them first.

3

Making It Happen

For the world to be interesting, you have to be manipulating it all the time.
(Brian Eno)

Having argued the point that creative liturgy should arise out of your own ideas and innovations, you probably need some insight into making and creating using some of the readily available tools out there, only some of which require mains electricity.

The mistake would be to assume that there is a monolith of technical skills which is needed before anything creative can be made. However, you learnt to walk through baby-steps, and you possibly learnt to play a musical instrument from simple tunes; and likewise you should experiment and build skills over time. I am constantly learning new techniques and learning from others. Often my next technical breakthrough is only made through either messing around until something interesting happens, or making the jump by trying to figure out how to achieve something. If this appears daunting at first, that is only because you are too worried about the whole mountain, rather than the foothill that is before you.

This chapter explores some technical aspects and discusses some good practice. I suggest you use it as a resource.

3.1 Projectors: Getting Your Message out There (on the Wall)

In the traditional Church of England, we seem to have lost our pre-Reformation love of the visual and the ritual, and nowhere is this more clearly seen than in the (mis)use of projectors.

My worst experience of projection occurred in a sacred space where one should have expected it to be slick and professional: a hugely successful charismatic Anglican church in a university town. There, amid impressive music, powerful testimony and the sight of dozens being baptized was the most second-rate use of a projector I have ever seen. For successful use of a projector does not rely on how much money you spend on kit but the thought and the preparation of what is displayed and the training and liturgical awareness of the operator.

The major error is one of distraction: Microsoft PowerPoint is a woefully inadequate tool for use in worship. Among its many issues, it provides the user with too many temptations to add frills, complex builds and transitions which only serve to distract rather than enhance the worship experience. You don't need any of these distractions. You don't need a cross, a waterfall, a sunset behind your words. You should use images where words are not needed, but if words are the important thing – use just words.

Similarly, you shouldn't use too many words. Many churches haven't grown out of their days with an OHP and acetates with two whole verses and a chorus on screen in very, very, very small writing.

Here are some bad examples. DO NOT ATTEMPT TO COPY THESE.

Above, the danger of distracting (and irrelevant) backgrounds, poor text contrast and too much text.

Immortal, invisible, God only wise,
in light inaccessible hid from our eyes,
most blessed, most glorious, the Ancient o
almighty, victorious, thy great name we pr(
Unresting, unhasting, and silent as light,
nor wanting, nor wasting, thou rulest in mig
thy justice like mountains high soaring abo
thy clouds which are fountains of goodness

Bad text contrast (on the CD you can see this in its glorious yellow on a bright green background which makes the viewer feel ill), the annoying Comic Sans font for which there is a special circle of hell reserved, and failing to get all the words on the screen.

Immortal, invisible, God only wise,
in light inaccessible hid from our eyes,
most blessed, most glorious, the Ancient of Days,
almighty, victorious, thy great name we praise.

Unresting, unhasting, and silent as light,
nor wanting, nor wasting, thou rulest in might;
thy justice like mountains high soaring above
thy clouds which are fountains of goodness and love.

To all, life thou givest, to both great and small;
in all life thou livest, the true life of all;
we blossom and flourish as leaves on the tree,
and wither and perish, but naught changeth thee.

Thou reignest in glory; thou dwellest in light;
thine angels adore thee, all veiling their sight;
all laud we would render: O help us to see
'tis only the splendor of light hideth thee.

This church clearly used to use an OHP and has not moved on: too much text, too small and a dull font which says nothing more than 'I don't know how to use this thing.'

My advice is to put no more than two lines of a hymn on the screen at any time and to fill the screen with it, so that it may be seen without a distracting background and in a simple clear font, such as Arial, Verdana, Tahoma, Helvetica (Mac) or Trebuchet.

Good Font Examples

Arial	abcdefghijklmnopqrstuvwxyz & ABCDEFGHIJKLMNOPRSTUVWXYZ
Verdana	abcdefghijklmnopqrstuvwxyz & ABCDEFGHIJKLMNOPRSTUVWXYZ
Tahoma	abcdefghijklmnopqrstuvwxyz & ABCDEFGHIJKLMNOPRSTUVWXYZ
Helvetica	abcdefghijklmnopqrstuvwxyz & ABCDEFGHIJKLMNOPRSTUVWXYZ
Trebuchet	abcdefghijklmnopqrstuvwxyz & ABCDEFGHIJKLMNOPRSTUVWXYZ

Bad Font examples

Comic Sans	abcdefghijklmnopqrstuvwxyz & ABCDEFGHIJKLMNOPRSTUVWXYZ
Times New Roman	abcdefghijklmnopqrstuvwxyz & ABCDEFGHIJKLMNOPRSTUVWXYZ
Brush Script	abcdefghijklmnopqrstuvwxyz & ABCDEFGHIJKLMNOPRSTUVWXYZ
Wingdings	♋♌♍♎♏♐♑♒♓ℋℯ&;●○■□□□□◆◆◆❖◆⊠⊡⌘ 📖 ✗✘♐♐✎✐✏🖊🖎☺☻☹💣☠🏱🏲✿◐❀❊✞✟✠✡✪☾

The operator cannot be allowed to fall asleep, but this is a good spur for teenagers for whom the Mass is otherwise the most boring thing ever – it keeps them alert because you have to change the slide before the end of the line, so you are up to speed with the text.

An example (hum along to the tune of St Denio):

Immortal, invisible,
God only wise,
in light inaccessible
hid from our eyes

Change here

most blessed,
most glorious,
the Ancient of Days,
almighty, victorious,
thy great name we
praise

Change here

I use simple visual clues, with responses in a different colour (usually red on a white background or yellow on a dark background):

The Lord be with you
and also with you

We probably all do something similar already with bold text in printed sheets, but instead throughout I always use yellow or red for congregation responses, and green for directions.

Homily
(let us be seated)

Or translations:

Miserere Nobis
(have mercy on us)

People unfamiliar with church find this simple 'Say the bright colour' approach easy to pick up and therefore less intimidating than wading through a booklet. It encourages singing and works very well with traditional hymnody.

3.2 Screens

I have never had the opportunity to design a sacred space from scratch, and so the challenge in planning liturgy in existing church spaces is to make the most of what is there and to minimize the challenges of the existing building. Many churches are hampered by pillars or other blocks to the line of sight, so the choice of screen position needs to take note of this. Rood screens can sometimes be used effectively, but care must be exercised as an inattentive crucifer can (literally!) bring the house down.

Some screen implementations can be very expensive, with motorized screens that can be brought down automatically, but these require professional fitting, and often permission. The solution lies in the moveable: At St Thomas the Apostle, Elson, we created an 8-feet-high trestle upon which a standard (and very cheap) projector screen is G-clamped. No special permissions are required for a moveable and temporary structure.

A compromise placing at St Thomas the Apostle, Elson: behind the action, and fully visible without obscuring traditional elements of the church.

A moveable trestle approximately 2 metres (6½ feet) high and a cheap screen. This screen can be moved easily, taken down or repositioned at will; and because it is moveable, the architectural police have no jurisdiction over it.[1]

The most effective position for projection is immediately behind the altar so that the screen does not distract from the focal liturgical activity, but rather encourages, points, focuses on the real liturgical action, as seen as Walsingham. This works well when you pull the altar into the nave as you can back-project from the chancel, but this does tend to annoy the choir.

---

1 In the Church of England, a body known as the Diocesan Advisory Committee for the Care of Churches (or DAC) safeguards churches from rash, permanent damage from ill-considered wholesale reordering. If the DACs had been in existence in Victorian times then they would have prevented the ruining of a good many medieval churches by the wanton installation of pews and organs. You might not have such a body in your church structure and can effectively do as you wish.

Above, a 'womb' created for an Advent Blesséd using lengths from a scaffolding tower and bits of cloth. We put projectors around the outside and projected the images, most notably the ultrasound of a foetus onto this womb-like structure.

Other solutions involve temporary hangings, banners, or even multiple projectors or LCD TVs, but I would counsel care that they do not become the focus of worship away from what is taking place on the altar. In a big space such as Walsingham, we concentrate during the consecration of the elements on the priest's hands and the elevation.

3.3 Projection Software

I have only one piece of advice in this area: don't use PowerPoint. It's like using a bicycle in the Isle of Man TT Races: you would get round, but only after a lot of wasted energy. It doesn't have the flexibility or the speed to display liturgy effectively. There are a number of applications that are available, ranging from open source (i.e. free) solutions such as DreamBeam through to very effective commercial applications such as MediaSout or my personal choice Easyworship.[2]

---

2 Open source software is not strictly free, but is licensed in a way which allows you to use it freely. The program code is made available for everyone and anyone can update or

Product	Cost	Comment
Dreambeam 0.81 <www.dreambeam.de>	Free	German, open source.[1]
SongView	Free	Very basic.
MediaShout 4	$429 Express: $249	Very comprehensive, popular but a bit complex.
Easyworship 2009	$399 Upgrade $99	Powerful yet simple interface.

A more detailed list can be found at <http://www.ebibleteacher.com/review worship.html>.[3]

What proper worship software offers is a complete integrated system for scripture, images, video and even web pages with the ability to respond dynamically to the worship environment which a linear system such as PowerPoint, even using presentation mode, cannot live up to.

In videos generally there are two distinct styles, philosophies even, which need to be noted:

The Visions style

Based in York, Visions is an alt.worship community which arose from the 1990s club scene. It uses video loops as an immersive process, as wallpaper around the scene (often using multiple screens) so the worshipper can just drop back and absorb the vibe from short, repetitive loops. The action of the priest often works independently of the screens.

The *Blesséd* style

Tends to use longer, less looped videos which drive forward the liturgy. They support direct liturgical action and have a distinct beginning and end. Usually based around a single screen, there is a partnership between priest and screen.

---

extend the program, submitting it back to the original author for inclusion. This makes the software very responsive to user needs as required features are swiftly developed, but it also means that software often lacks finesse or documentation or help. Some find that unacceptable, and prefer commercial software that has these things, but which only develops as the vendors wish it to. I have a sense that open source software is fundamentally a more Christian software solution: users help each other and problems are often resolved by return of email directly from the author in my experience.

3 Accessed 17 February 2010.

Both styles have validity, but move in different directions. As you develop your own sacramental worship, you might find yourself growing in one direction or the other.

3.4 Creating Videos

3.4.1 Cutting the Video

This phrase seems increasing anachronistic when no real film is actually cut, unlike the olden days of film editing, but pixel-bashing has yet to become an acceptable alternative.

In addition to your video-editing package, you might need to prepare and trim your footage. One free and powerful tool is VideoDub,[4] which can be used to cut sections out of a longer video and save them separately. It can be complex to configure, but its basic operation is quite straightforward.

3.4.2 Video Editing

Feature films shown in the cinema such as *Cold Mountain* are edited digitally on an Apple Macintosh computer, and there is a plethora of video-editing products available, some of which are supplied in the Windows or Macintosh Operating System.

Product	Cost	Comment
Windows Movie Maker (PC)	Free	Comes as standard. Basic but easy. Under Windows 7, you can now download this free as a part of the Windows Live Essentials pack at <http://download.live.com/>.
iMovie (Mac)	Free if your Mac is bundled with iWork package	Comes as standard. Basic but easy.

---

4 <http://www.dvdvideosoft.com/products/dvd/Free-Video-Dub.htm>.

Adobe Premiere Elements 7	£53.00	Mix of complex and wizards to help home users. Limited video layers.
Adobe Premiere CS4	£500	Professional.
Sony Vegas Studio 9	£28	Only four layers of video but very powerful still.
Sony Vegas Pro 9	$600	Professional.

3.4.3 Walkthrough: Creating a Simple Video in Windows Movie Maker – the Angelus

The DVD contains the basic sound track and images to use in this walkthrough in <drive>:\resources\angelus where <drive> is the letter of your computer's DVD drive. This video serves as a good introduction because of its simplicity. It was one of the first videos I ever created, all because it met a need – we didn't have a bell to ring the Angelus.

Windows Movie Maker can be downloaded free as a part of the Windows Live Essentials pack from <http://download.live.com/>. Once installed, it is available on your Start Menu.

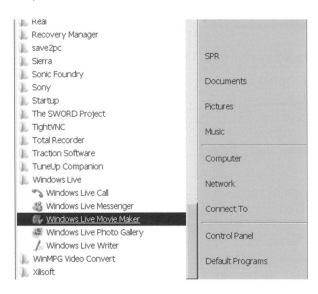

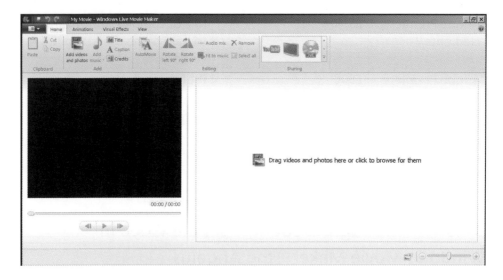

This is the main Movie Maker window.

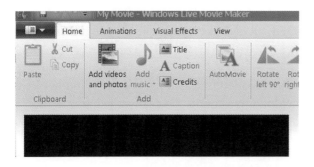

To begin, you need to import your images from the DVD. Click on **Add Videos and Photos**.

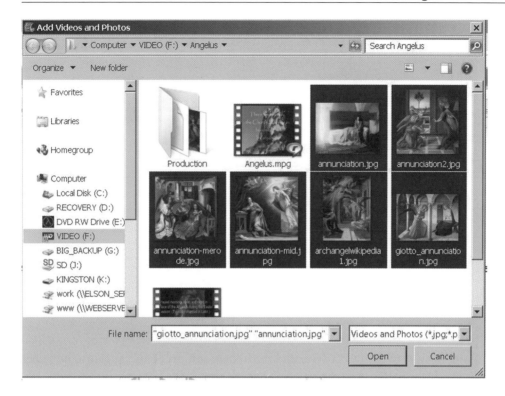

Browse to your DVD drive, select the **resources** folder and inside that you will find the **angelus** folder. Highlight all the images files which end in **.jpg** and select **Open**.

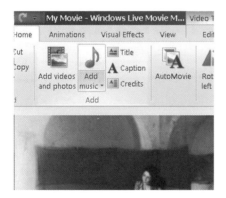

To add an audio track, select from the taskbar **Add Music**.

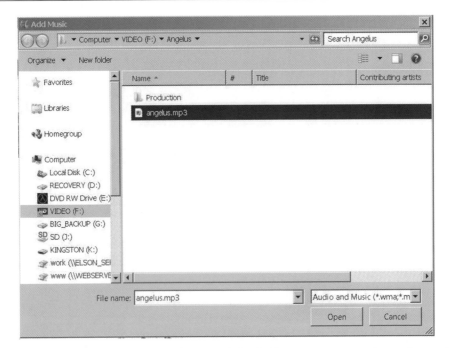

Again, browse to the DVD drive and the folders **resources** and **angelus** and select the **angelus.mp3** file. Select **Open** to confirm that is the file you wish to add.

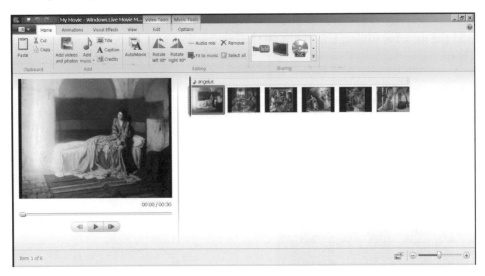

You will now see the images lined up in the timeline and the audio placed above it. If you chose to add the images one by one, then you can change the preferred order as you add them, or you can swap their positions by simply clicking and rearranging them.

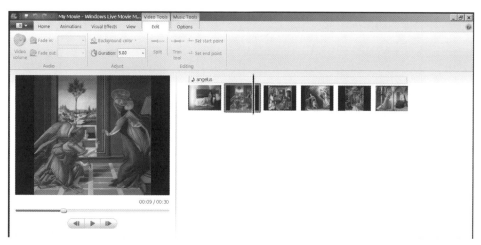

You can preview the video so far by pressing the **play** button below the preview screen. You will see the images of the annunciation displayed and the images simply changing from one to the next after about five seconds. However, it doesn't match the music, so we want to change the length of each picture to match the music. If you play the sequence, you will see that the first image change needs to be at **13 seconds**.

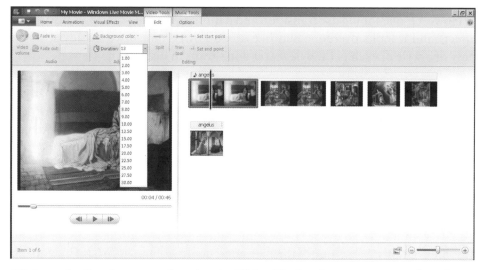

Click on the first image, and under the **Video Tools** tab, you can see a dropdown box for **Duration**. You could select a pre-defined duration, or in this case, simply type **13** into the **Duration** box to set the length of the first image to **13 seconds**. You will see the length of the image increase in length to represent the increase in duration. Repeat this for each image to match the duration of each image to each toll of the bell on the audio track.

To make the changes between images a little more interesting, select from the **Animations** menu any of the effects for changing from one image to another (transition). You can also add panning and zooming effects to each image which can draw further attention to the image. Double-clicking on the effect will add it to the movie.

However, one should use transition and panning/zooming sparingly: too many effects and it looks overdone and like a bad PowerPoint. I would advise using only one style of each per movie if you don't want to distract the viewer.

To save your movie, go to the **Home** menu and under the **Sharing** section you can see three options. Select one of them. A good quality of movie for use in worship would be the **DVD** settings.

You will be asked where you want to save the movie in the format you selected. I usually save it in a separate folder along with the images and video I have used. This means they remain on hand in one place should I wish to change this video in the future.

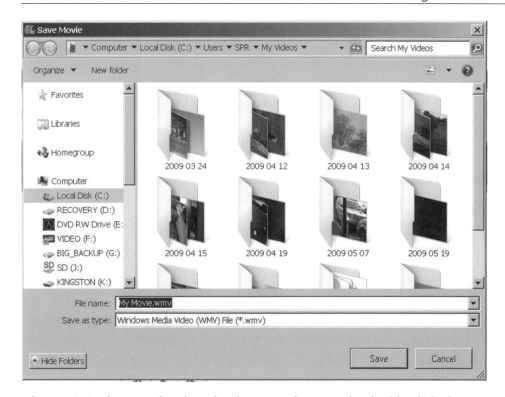

The movie is then 'rendered' and, when complete, can be double-clicked on to view.

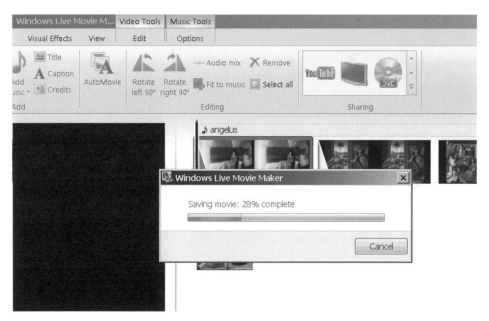

A typical movie can be quite large: too large to be easily emailed. A four-minute video might be as big as 30Mb in size. If you want to show someone the video you have made by email, then it is best to upload it to a movie-sharing site such as YouTube or Vimeo. If you want to show it in church in decent quality then save the video to a memory stick, a portable hard-drive or burn it onto a DVD.

3.4.4 Walkthrough: Creating a Simple Video in Mac iMovie – the Angelus

The DVD contains the basic sound track and images to use in this walkthrough in dvd:resources:angelus.

The iMovie application can found on the taskbar at the bottom of the main Mac screen.

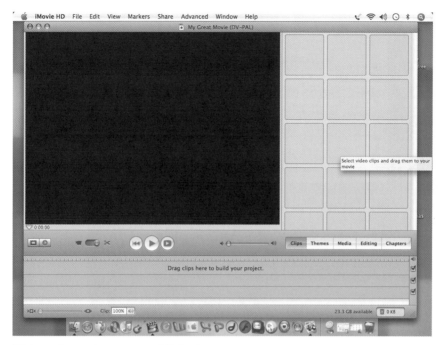

This is the main screen of iMovie.

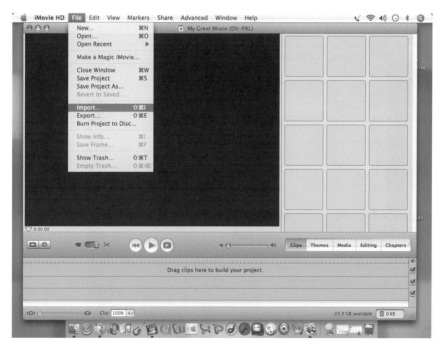

To add images and sounds, select from the **File** menu **Import.**

You can browse to the DVD, and inside the **resources** and then **angelus** folders you will find the images to use in this movie. Alternatively, you can drag and drop images into the library on the right-hand side of the screen. Select as many **.jpg** images as you wish to use and the **angelus.mp3** sound clip.

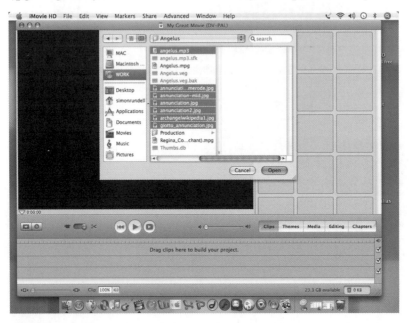

The images and sounds will then be imported.

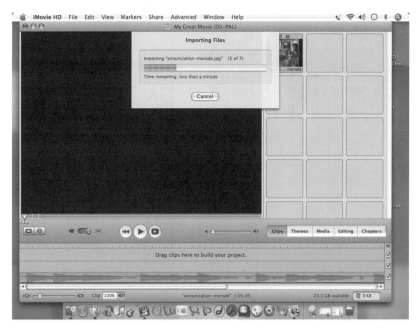

If it has not been imported automatically, drag and drop the audio onto the time-line at the bottom. You can see the waveform of the sound illustrated.

Then drag and drop the images onto the timeline in the order in which you wish to display them.

If you do not see the waveform, check that the little clock is selected.

By default, each image is shown for five seconds. We need to make this longer to fit the sound. To do this, take the cursor to the right-hand edge of the picture on the timeline, so that the cursor changes, hold down the mouse button and drag the mouse to the right. This click and drag procedure enables you to drag the image to the correct duration (about 13 seconds).

The first image now fits the first three tolls of the bell.

Repeat with each image, moving them to fit each of the waveforms. Match their lengths visually to the waveform.

To make each of the transitions between images more interesting, select the **Transitions** tab on the right-hand side. You can drag and drop any of the transitions between images.

To create the finished movie, select **Share** on the menu, and the quality of the output you wish to create. A good quality of movie for use in worship would be the **Quicktime** settings.

You are then asked what to call the movie and where to save it.

The movie is then converted into a usable format, which is known as *rendering*. A video of sufficient quality to be used in worship can be around 30Mb for a four-minute movie. This is too large to be emailed to anyone. Should you wish to share a video, then I suggest uploading to a video-sharing site such as YouTube or Vimeo. To transport such movies around, I suggest using memory sticks or portable hard-drives.

3.4.5 File Formats, Codecs and Compression

The two previous sections for Mac or PC offer some standard file formats for use in your worship. There are hundreds of formats available and some of them require extra software, known as *codecs*, to enable them to play on your machine. Over time, new codecs appear offering higher compression (i.e. smaller file sizes) with better quality images.

You should always strive to be able to use the highest quality in worship that your machinery can comfortably play. If you use too large a file, then the PC or Mac will become slow and unstable. You should experiment with different settings to obtain the best usable quality and recognize that this will always be a trade-off.

If the video compression is too high, or the quality selected too poor, the video will look blocky, especially when projected onto a screen; the audio will appear garbled. Videos downloaded directly from YouTube and played direct to screen can often look a little 'overcompressed' in this way.

Thankfully there is an acceptable lowest common denominator format for videos which can play out of the box with no additional software on *both* PCs and Macs. This file format is called MPG-1 and is often referred to as *VideoCD* format. MPG-1 can be burnt to a CD or DVD and will play in most standard household DVD players, which is the ultimate fallback position when all the other technology fails.

A higher quality codec which makes very good quality movies at a very reasonable size is the MPEG-4 standard (also referred to as H.264) which is very effective for HD-quality videos and is a standard used on Blu-ray disks.

3.5 Copyright and Licensing

Copyright laws vary from country to country. In the UK, an item is copyrighted if the creator or content owner (not necessarily the same thing, sadly) asserts their right. The copyright remains in force for 50 years for sound recordings and broadcasts or 70 years for literary, dramatic, musical or other artistic works. There have been some attempts by artists and their estates to extend that duration, so this time limit might in future rise even further.

3.5.1 Copyright

The problem with copyright is not that it seeks to provide the artist with recompense for their endeavours; it does serve to ensure that artists (visual or musical) do not get ripped off mercilessly. It also has a downside: it shores up a model of restrictive practice and stifles further creativity.

Artists have throughout the ages been influenced by their predecessors, borrowing techniques and compositions, and even in the case of Shakespeare, plotlines that were well known in his age. The Dada movement of the early twentieth century began to use ephemeral materials: newspapers, advertisements and all kinds of multimedia materials in new (and shocking) creative works. Pop Art sought to appropriate the mundane and elevate it to the gallery: Warhol's Campbells Soup Cans is a good example; and so now modern artists seek to take what exists within their grasp (as delivered to them by the internet) and transform it into new forms of creativity. Video and imagery are manipulated into new shapes, sound is borrowed and remixed, pixels are reformed and transformed from their original shape. This new burst of adaptive creativity is touching the worlds of art, music and film in transformative ways, and it reaches, I would argue, the peak of its expression in the creativity that embodies all of these: the worship of Almighty God.

Speaking personally, the gospel is more important than any law, and honouring God comes before financially honouring any person. I inhabit a culture where intellectual property is seen not as an end product but as a tool for further enhancement: the growth of sampling or the mashup video and the development of the download as the key method of music distribution in the past two years has reflected modern youth's disregard of copyright as a concept and the embracing of other forms of intellectual property which ensure proper attribution, reasonable recompense and creative freedom. Sharing files is not seen as a crime by young people.

Having said that, we should respect an individual's creativity, and provide suitable recompense for their God-given talents. Copyright at present is one of the few solutions to this complex problem, although new solutions are in development which can reward content creators and their distributors.[5] Thankfully the Performing Rights Society think the same as I do: they have stated that they will not pursue copyright on a creative work if it is being used in an act of divine worship for which no charge is being made.[6]

These new forms of expression – the remix, the mashup and the creative worship – fundamentally challenge the old structure of copyright, which proves quite

5 Flattr: an innovative micropayment solution from one of the originators of the Pirate Bay. See <www.flattr.com>, accessed 16 February 2010.

6 <http://www.prsformusic.com/users/businessesandliveevents/musicforbusinesses/charityandcommunity/Pages/default.aspx>, accessed 23 December 2009. 'We do not make a charge for music used as part of divine worship. We also make no charge for music used as part of wedding ceremonies, civil wedding and partnership ceremonies, funerals or in funeral homes.'

inadequate for the purpose. New ways of use and reuse are required. One such new solution is Creative Commons.

3.5.2 Creative Commons

Copyright is only one solution to issues of ownership. A new form of user rights has arisen over the past few years with the explicit aim of sharing material that may be used, extended and given back: the Creative Commons Licence.

> With Creative Commons, the act of creation becomes not the end, but the beginning of a creative process that links complete strangers together in collaboration. (Jonathan Coulton, musician)[7]

The Creative Commons licence recognizes that other people's creativity can enhance and build upon what you create. It is a licensing model that lends itself readily to internet-based collaboration. Full information and assistance on setting the right licence for your work can be found at <www.creativecommons. org>.

3.5.2.1 Creative Commons License Conditions

Creators choose a set of conditions that they wish to apply to their work.

(i) Attribution

You let others copy, distribute, display and perform your copyrighted work – and derivative works based upon it – but only if they give credit the way you request.

(o) Share Alike

You allow others to distribute derivative works only under a licence identical to the licence that governs your work.

(s) Non-commercial

You let others copy, distribute, display and perform your work – and derivative works based upon it – but for non-commercial purposes only.

---

7 http://creativecommons.org, accessed 23 December 2009.

No Derivative Works

You let others copy, distribute, display and perform only verbatim copies of your work, not derivative works based upon it.

3.5.2.2 The Licences

 Attribution

This licence lets others distribute, remix, tweak and build upon your work, even commercially, as long as they credit you for the original creation. This is the most accommodating of licences offered, in terms of what others can do with your works licensed under Attribution.

 Attribution Share Alike

This licence lets others remix, tweak and build upon your work even for commercial reasons, as long as they credit you and licence their new creations under the identical terms. This licence is often compared to open source software licences. All new works based on yours will carry the same licence, so any derivatives will also allow commercial use.

 Attribution No Derivatives

This licence allows for redistribution, commercial and non-commercial, as long as it is passed along unchanged and in whole, with credit to you.

 Attribution Non-Commercial

This licence lets others remix, tweak and build upon your work non-commercially, and although their new works must also acknowledge you and be non-commercial, they don't have to licence their derivative works on the same terms.

Attribution Non-Commercial Share Alike

This licence lets others remix, tweak and build upon your work non-commercially, as long as they credit you and license their new creations under the identical terms. Others can download and redistribute your work just like the by Non-Commercial No Derivatives licence (below), but they can also translate, make remixes and produce new stories based on your work. All new work based on yours will carry the same licence, so any derivatives will also be non-commercial in nature.

 Attribution Non-Commercial No Derivatives

This licence is the most restrictive of the six main licences, allowing redistribution. This licence is often called the 'free advertising' license because it allows others to download your works and share them with others as long as they mention you and link back to you, but they can't change them in any way or use them commercially.

3.5.3 Public Domain

Some materials may be freely available. A work in the public domain is free for everyone to use without asking for permission or paying royalties. The phrase 'public domain' is a copyright term referring to works that belong to the public. Works can be in the public domain for a variety of reasons: because the term of copyright protection has expired; because the work was not eligible for copyright protection in the first place; or because the copyright owner has given the copyright in the work to the public domain. Often videos placed on sites like YouTube by their creators are considered to have been placed in the Public Domain.

However, one must exercise a little caution, as a photograph of a public statue or of an Old Master painting which is publicly owned as an artwork might in itself be copyrighted.

3.5.4 Getting a Still Image onto Your Machine

This does very much depend upon your browser and type of machine.

First, let us use Google Images to find a suitable image. Go to <http://images.google.com>.

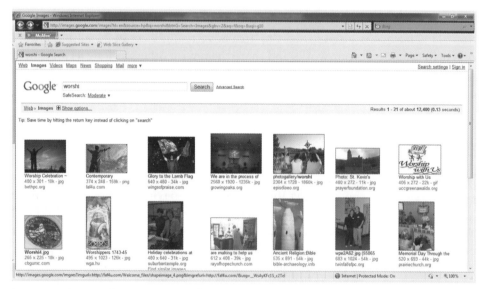

Enter a suitable search term. The better the search term you enter, the better result you are likely to get. Try a number of searches and don't just accept the first thing shown to you.

Your results are shown in a window similar to the above. Click on the image you are interested in. You can see the image in context which will help you decide if it is useful to you.

See full size image

374 x 248 - 159k - png - faf4u.com/Welcome_files/shapeimage_4.png
Image may be subject to copyright.
Below is the image at: faf4u.com/

Click on **See full size image** to get the picture alone shown in your browser. You might be browsing the internet and see an image you like and want to use. From here, it all depends on the browser you are using.

3.5.4.1 PC and Internet Explorer

If you don't know what kind of browser you are using, it's fairly safe to assume you are using Internet Explorer.

Once you have found an image you want, select it by right-clicking on the image and selecting **Save Picture As ...**

You will be asked where to save it, and if you wish, you can give it a different name. This might help you in searching for it later, especially if the name of the image is machine generated, intentionally obscure or just plain unhelpful, i.e. 'picture1.jpg'.

3.5.4.2 PC and Mozilla Firefox

You will probably know if you are using Firefox, which can be downloaded for free from <http://www.mozilla-europe.org/en/firefox/>. This is a much better browser than Internet Explorer. It is faster, more robust and less vulnerable to security issues than its main rival.

Accessing an image via Google Images is the same as above, but when you right-click on an image, you should select **Save Image As ...**

3.5.4.3 PC and Google Chrome

Chrome is another latest-generation browser which is very fast and closely integrated with the Google search engine. It can be downloaded for free from: <http://www.google.com/chrome>. This is my browser of choice because it is light and fast, and you can search Google simply by typing your search term into the address bar at the top.

Accessing an image via Google Images is entirely the same as above, but when you right-click on an image, you should select **Save Image As ...**

3.5.4.4 Mac and Safari

If you are a Mac user and have no idea what browser you are using, then you will find it is called Safari. Accessing an image via Google Images is entirely the same as above, but when you right-click on an image, you should select **Save Image As ...**

3.5.4.5 Mac and Other Browsers

Almost all other browsers available for Mac follow the same processes as described above. This is a very good thing about the Mac: consistency of approach.

3.6 Video Resources

The DVD that comes with this book contains a wealth of video footage which can be incorporated into your own worship. Some of the footage has been heavily used by *Blesséd*, while other material has been filmed especially for your own use. However, very quickly you will discover that these materials are inadequate and you will need to find other images and footage to support your wonderfully creative ideas.

3.6.1 Video from the Internet

The broadband revolution has meant that a content-rich, video-saturated internet is now the norm, which provides lots of opportunity to find the perfect shot.

3.6.2 Searching

YouTube <www.youtube.com> is certainly the most prolific video-sharing site on the internet, with millions of hours of footage being uploaded weekly.[8] Among the material (some placed there illegally, and usually taken down very rapidly, others placed there by the copyright-owner to raise publicity), there is a lot of material which is shot by users and effectively placed into the public domain. As with a lot of user-generated content, the quality varies widely in terms of video quality (camera phones are very popular), shot quality and labelling. One simply needs to be patient and use a variety of search terms to find the right images.

Vimeo <http://www.vimeo.com> is another video-sharing site which attracts more dedicated videophiles as users: one can upload longer and higher quality (bigger) videos, and so quality and labelling tend to be more accurate. Sometimes fewer, better quality hits for your search engine can be more productive.

Google Video <http://video.google.com> is the Google search engine optimized for finding videos from all over the internet, and aggregates the contents

---

8 <http://www.youtube.com/t/fact_sheet>, accessed 16 February 2010. They claim that 20 hours of footage are uploaded every minute. Something must fit the bill!

of YouTube, Vimeo and many other sites. It is my practice to resort to Google Video after YouTube and Vimeo have proved unsatisfactory.

The Internet Movie Archive (<http://www.archive.org>) is a public domain archive of many interesting and useful films, now available freely. Many documentaries, public information films and older works are archived there, and the IMA has the added advantage of providing the clips for download in an already useable format.

Although the BBC iPlayer enables the user to download BBC material to your machine for offline viewing, this file is technically protected from reuse in your video-making efforts. A search on the internet may in time reveal methods for circumventing this and downloading a protection-free file.

3.6.3 Downloading

The problem is that most videos on the internet, and especially those found on the principal video sharing sites Youtube and Vimeo, appear in a highly compressed format based upon Adobe Flash: the .flv format. Few video-editing packages can interpret the .flv format and so one needs a utility program to download and convert the video into something useful. These download programs may be standalone applications, usually at a minimal cost; or one could use an online convertor such as that provided freely at <vixy.net>.

Type	Application	Cost	Advantages	Disadvantages
Standalone	Save2PC www.save2pc.com	$34 Free version for YouTube only	Can download from many sites, including Youtube, Google Video and Vimeo.	PC only.
Web based	Vixy.net	Free		Youtube only, can be used by different types of machine (PC and Mac).

As with finding still images for use in worship, finding the right video clip is highly dependent upon your choice of search terms, your willingness to keep searching with different terms, and use of a video editor to pull from the raw video the right section of video from a download. It is indeed rare to find a complete video which will meet your needs perfectly, but each video will probably need trimming, framing or incorporation to make it useful. One should not accept the first image that matches your key words searched for.

Another solution to the format problem is to use a video conversion utility. Many of these are free, or of minimal cost.

Application	Cost	Advantages	Disadvantages
Super Download from <http://www.erightsoft.org/ GetFile.php?SUPERsetup.exe>	Free	It is free and it works well.	Very poor website which makes it very difficult to find the link to download an upgrade.
Daniosoft Media Converter <http://www.daniusoft. com/>	Ultimate $59.95 Pro $39.95	30-day trial. Excellent range of formats.	Expensive.
WinMPG <http://www.winmpg.com/>	$20	Works well for low-cost application.	

3.6.4 Video from Your Camera

The perfect image might be in your midst, in your church or among your youth group. There are times when images which are recognizable in your community are highly desirable. Multi-megapixel video cameras are now very cheap (under £150). Some cameras can record directly onto a memory card and therefore be imported directly into your PC or Mac.

At that price, one can easily hand such a camera to young people, and ask them to film things: images of your community actually worshipping can be useful. However, there is usually a tendency to use the zoom function, which should be avoided as it makes people feel sick: *film, stop, reframe, film* will make more useful shots. Shots should fill the frame where possible as these can draw the eye most readily; again many inexperienced shooters of film tend to hang back and fail to get close enough to the subject to see what is being seen: background is generally bad. The bigger and the closer, the better.

3.6.5 Screen Grabbing

Sometimes, the only solution for accessing images and video is to capture a small part of your screen. A number of applications exist to capture a window or a part of a screen, such as the powerful Traction Software's Screen Grab Pro (<http://www.traction-software.co.uk/screengrabpro/>) which is free.

The most basic form of screen grab will capture the entire screen and comes with your computer.

On a Mac, to capture the entire desktop, press **Command-Shift-3**. The screen shot will be automatically saved as a PNG file on your desktop. To capture a portion of the screen use **Command-Shift-4**.

On a PC, press the **Print Screen** key on your keyboard. It may be labelled (**PrtScn**). This will copy the image to the clipboard so that you can paste it into your chosen application.

3.7 Sounds: Drawing on Your Record Collection (or Your Hard Disk, or Spotify ...)

You already love music. Don't try and deny it. Whatever age you are at, whatever stage in life you find yourself, you have been moved by music. It may have been Palestrina or Purcell, it may have been the Beatles or Led Zeppelin, it might have been Joy Division or the Smiths, or, as in my case, it might have been a combination of all of these.

Your music, and the music of your community, already speaks volumes for you. It has already been the soundtrack to your life,[9] and it should therefore be the soundtrack to your worship. If it speaks to you emotionally, it already speaks to you of God. Some alt.worship communities such as Visions were born directly out of a clubbing scene, and so their particular style of ambient hardbag mixed with church classics speaks wonderfully of them and their approach to God.

---

9 D. Jones (2006), *iPod therefore I am*, London: Phoenix; also G. Smith (2004), *Lost in Music*, London: Picador. The single best book about being a music fan ever written.

Beyond that, the music of Brian Eno,[10] of Sigur Ros,[11] of Massive Attack[12] seems to lend itself to this kind of work. You might not have heard of them before. It might be time to seek them out on Spotify (<www.spotify.com> – a music-streaming service supported by advertising or subscription – which is an ideal way to encounter music before you buy it).

One creative approach is to gather your community together and play 'soul music' – to bring music which moves you to others. Some may dislike intensely what you bring, but even that reaction should be seen as a creative one, for we are a product of both what we love and what we dislike.[13] To play a piece of music to my peers and try and explain why it moves me, to explore my *Desert Island Discs*, is to speak of that which moves our very souls and can be a very spiritual experience.

If we hold everything to be sacred and nothing to be profane, then all musical styles and genres are available for use in worship. For centuries it was held that God always wanted music that was stylistically about 100 years behind popular music: Bach wrote in a style which was deliberately old-fashioned because the popular vernacular was simply too brash for sacred music. If all of creation belongs to God, then all creativity, all techniques, all styles can reflect the glory of God.

In the next chapter we will provide examples of liturgy which seek to speak in creative ways of God and of his goodness. When you merge them with your own creativity and ideas, then wonderful things will be expressed of God.

---

10 Roxy Music, and then to experimental electronic music.

11 Possibly the most interesting band of the age: an Icelandic group who sing such poignant music in a language which is no language and experiment in such diverse areas and yet whose music manages to uplift the soul.

12 Bristol-based group who manage to make 'no two records the same': such creativity within the dance-music genre.

13 There is a marvellous scene in the seminal film *Human Traffic* where this happens.

4

Creative Examples

You will probably have bought this book just for this section, which is ironic as the most important message you should get is, *make your own*. Use the following texts as sources, but above all, create innovative liturgy from this inspiration.

The shape of Eucharistic Liturgy remains constant throughout. Our blank piece of paper always begins with these headings:

Gathering	Open ended, beginning before the advertised time, and drifting the people towards time for worship, which *always* begins right on time as advertised
Introduction	In the name of ... Words to set the scene
Penitential Rite	Seeking forgiveness
Absolution	Receiving forgiveness
Gloria	Sheer unadulterated worship – a response to the forgiveness of sins
Collect – opening prayer	Prayer of the theme
Word	Scripture
Gospel	Essential scripture
Homily	Some kind of reflection or response to the scripture. Most emphatically *not* a 45–minute exposition of the text
Creed	Affirmation of faith
Intercessions	Let us pray ... most often visual in nature

Offering	Giving to God
Eucharistic Prayer	The heart of the matter
Preface	Theme of the Mass
Sanctus and Benedictus	The words of the angels
Epiclesis	The invocation of the Holy Spirit
Institution	Recalling the words and actions of Christ at the Last Supper
Anaphora	Giving thanks alongside the whole company of heaven, for this Mass is but a reflection of the Eucharist continually being offered before God[1]
Lord's Prayer	As our Saviour taught us …
Agnus Dei	Recalling the words of John and the sacrificial nature of the Mass
Communion	Bread, wine, salvation
Post-Communion Prayer	Sum it all up
Blessing	God's gift to us
Dismissal	… now go out and make it real *Ite Missa Est* Go, the Mass is ended

Now, go and fill in the blanks!

4.1 Gathering

Gathering is a key part of the Eucharist. It is not simply the rehearsing of the band, a couple of quick notices[2] before the entrance of the ministers. It is a time for pulling in and reflecting, a time of spiritual preparation. If that needs to be a

---

1 Revelation 5.

2 The beginning of the Mass is *never* the right place for notices, which should be prayerful and reflective. Leave them until after the Post-Communion Prayer. The sign posted in many churches which says 'Talk to God before Mass; talk to each other after Mass' has some legitimacy.

mixture of quietness and expectancy or lively music to set a tone, then it should be seen as important, not an afterthought. In some places, people have walked to church for hours, their time of arrival uncertain, and so the gathering process may be elongated, and the Mass starts when that gathering has concluded – preferably at the exact moment that the Mass time is advertised, for we owe it to the people to begin when we say we will. Late is just disrespectful to them.

Blesséd's gatherings all inevitably start with music and image. Powerful musical choices such as Michael Nyman's 'MGV', Sabres of Paradise – 'Smokebelch II' (beatless mix). Images have ranged from stills, pans across Google Earth (grabbed from a screen capture program[3]) and sequences from the stunning films in the *Qatsi Trilogy*[4] directed by Godfrey Reggio with film score by Philip Glass.

4.2 The Penitential Rite

4.2.1 Bittersweet

Acknowledging the influence of Jonny Baker, this ritual took a decidedly *Blesséd* mutation. Set to 'Bittersweet Symphony' by the Verve.
    Introduction:

Life is complex and hard. Life is challenging and not without its fair share of pain. The preacher on TV who offers you untold riches, health, wealth, healing and joy has clearly never read the book of Job.

Life is beautiful and delicate. Life is filled with joy and laughter. The glass which was created by God is always at least half-full, beyond half-full, and closer to full to overflowing.

To see life as either one or the other is to miss the point of life in all its rollercoaster of variety. We learn in life to take the bitter and the sweet.

Around this sacred space are six stations, where you may taste in the lemon the bitterness of life, where you can offer to God in penitence those difficult, trying, hard things in your life. You may also taste a spoonful of honey – to *taste and see that the Lord is good* as the Psalmist said, and to give thanks to God for his many, many blessings.

---

3 See 3.6.5, 'Screen grabbing', above.
4 Koyaanisqatsi (Life out of Balance), Powaqqatsi (Life in Transformation) and Naqoyatsi (Life as War).

Without one, there is no other. Without both, life is meaningless. Offer them both to God in penitence and faith, and let us now be reconciled to God.

Stations: four or six stations with a balti dish of lemons (and a bin) and a dish of honey with small spoons to taste a lemon and a spoon of honey.
Each station has text by it:

Station with lemons:

Taste the bitterness of life.
Without this, the sweet,
good times are nothing.

Give to God the pain, the
sadness and the hurt.

Taste and see that the Lord is good.

Station with honey:

Taste the sweetness of life.
Without this, the bitter,
ugly, hard times become
everything.

Give thanks to God for the joy,
the pleasure and the laughs.
Taste and see that the Lord is good.

At both stations:

In happy moments, praise God.
In difficult moments, seek God.
In quiet moments, worship God.
In painful moments, trust God.
In every moment, thank God.

4.2.2 Cup of Suffering

Take a chalice, and put into it red wine vinegar. Place it on the altar or at a station where the individual partaking of the cup is facing away from the queue of people still to undertake the ritual.

Come and drink from the cup …

The cup of suffering.

The cup of suffering may be of our own making, our own issues, or the issues of the world.

If you want to walk the way of Christ then you are called to drink from the cup of suffering.

That's what it takes to obey God, he told James and John. He tells us.

Even Christ himself paused, and asked God if this cup might not pass from him, but still, he accepted it readily.

Will you take from the cup that our Lord took from?

Many will take from the chalice imagining it to be like Holy Communion; for many, the bitter taste of wine vinegar will be a complete shock. The same kind of shock as for the disciples, I suspect. Dare we taste from the same cup as our Lord? Most of us ignore the challenge inherent in the Passion.

4.2.3 Advent Confession

We confess that we no longer wait for you, God
or the love that comes in your name.
We no longer eagerly anticipate the advent
of hope or joy or peace.
Because the disappointment is too great when you don't turn up.
We wonder why you can't make a better plan than this,
something a little less risky
and a little more foolproof.

We confess …

Our cynicism.
Our fear.
Our doubt.

And with what little faith we have left,
we pray you will wrap them with forgiveness
born of infinite love and compassion.

**May today be the day that we find you,
may today be the day that you come.**

Amen.

(Cheryl Lawrie[5]
<www.holdthisspace.au>)

4.2.4 Advent Light

I lit candles and the room was bathed in warm light.
The outside remained dark and cold.
There was this moth – thirsty for a fix of light.
Desperate to throw herself at the light without considered consequence.
She drummed relentlessly on the window pane …
Time and time again.
Time and time again.
Time and time again.
Exhausted.
I opened the window.
In she came, she drew near, waited and rested …
Don't give up searching and longing for the light … Advent is near.

(Ron Cole[6]
<www.thewearypilgrim.com>)

---

5 With kind permission of the author.
6 With kind permission of the author.

4.2.5 Paper

There is something concrete about the confession process when we see our written confessions destroyed permanently. The writing makes our sin tangible, and its destruction shows us powerfully the power of Christ over sin. The following ritual can take two forms: the first uses a special paper called 'Flash paper' and is used by magicians: a touch of flame and it rapidly disintegrates, leaving no trace, and it cannot fail to impress. Flash paper is building-safe and can even be held as it burns, although some care is advised. We invite people to write their sins on a small piece of flash paper and then place them in a balti dish for burning. This is very dramatic.

The second solution uses another special paper called 'Dissolvo' – a paper which dissolves completely and rapidly in water. It is sold by magic/joke shops, sometimes as 'spy paper'. Again, the congregation are invited to confess their sins, and then the paper is placed in water. We have effectively used an ancient font for this. It works best if the water flows, and so the addition of a portable pump from an aquarium or a bathside jacuzzi blower makes the streams of living water[7] flow. As the paper meets the water it dissolves completely and the link between the waters of Baptism and Absolution is made plain. On one occasion, when this ritual was undertaken at a Mass outside, people did it collectively rather than one at a time, and for a split second we were treated to the vision of the paper dissolved and the (unintelligible) felt-pen writing hanging in the water before being dispersed: a truly powerful evocation of what Christ does for our sins.

> There are many things that we would like to discard,
> to throw away and have nothing more to do with.
>
> There are many things that we feel are not worthy of us
> and need to be put aside.
>
> Write down something you want deeply to throw away:
> a behaviour,
> an action,
> a word said in haste,
> a relationship gone bad,
> a deed undone,
> an obligation unfulfilled.

---

7 John 4.14.

and give it over to God.

You can pour out your heart to God on the mountaintop.
You can painfully trace each step in the darkness of the confessional.
You can say the words we know so well without thinking.
But have you written him a love letter?
Have you given what you want to throw away to God?
Let God deal with your deepest fears and shame.

Write down something you want deeply to throw away:
a behaviour,
an action,
a word said in haste,
a relationship gone bad,
a deed undone,
an obligation unfulfilled.

And give it over to God.

There are many things that we would like to discard,
to throw away and have nothing more to do with.

There are many things that we feel are not worthy of us,
and need to be put aside

Put them aside, and give them to God.

For God will transform,
and the shameful past becomes the bright future.

4.2.6 Kneed Forgiveness

The tactile is one of the least used of our senses in worship, and yet as multisensory creations we are called to use all of them in reaching out to God. The penitential rite, used most effectively during a Harvest Festival in a general church setting, enabled us to work our messy lives into this dough. The dough was then discarded, but at the same time a loaf of bread was baked in a breadmaker and timed to be ready at the Offertory, filling the church with the wonderful smell of fresh bread. It could not be the same dough, as a breadmaker takes about three hours, and there is a hygiene issue, but in our minds the link is made, and God consecrates the (small portion) of that loaf for the Eucharist, and our sins are transformed into salvation.

Suggested music for this ritual (and the one before it) is 'Ceramic Avenue' by Brian Eno and Andy Partridge. This piece of music is slow, rhythmic and of a simple beauty which lends itself to this kind of penitential ritual.

> From shapeless forms rise something new.
> From warm wet dough, comes living bread.
> From running our hands over this Mass
> a new Mass is moulded.
>
> Into this bread we work our lives.
> Into this dough we place our struggles and failures.
> Right through this material
> we seed our sins
> and give it to God.
>
> For yeast and heat and air and flour are taken by God and transformed
> and the invisible hand of God gives rise to the yeast.
>
> So too are we transformed.
>
> And we rise, we rise, we rise with the Son
> in the warmth of his love,
> the scent of his holiness,
> the wonder of his creation.
>
> And it will rise
> and be overcome.

4.2.7 Absolution

No penitential rite is complete without absolution. We have sometimes illustrated authorized words with fireworks and images of the dawn to show a new beginning, or at its starkest, the declaration on the screen 'You are forgiven' makes it plain as the priest makes good Christ's promises.

I have been drawn at times to use congregationally the form of absolution often given in the Book of Common Prayer's 'Visitation of the Sick' and at the end of the private Sacrament of Reconciliation, especially as they contain the important entreaty at the end, 'Pray for me, a sinner also', which humbly reminds the priest of his or her role in this.

> Screen: **You are forgiven**.
> Our Lord Jesus Christ, who has left power to his Church to
> absolve all sinners who truly repent and believe in him, of
> his great mercy forgive you all your offences; and by his
> authority committed to me, I absolve you from all your sins:
> In the name of the +Father, and of the Son, and of the Holy
> Spirit.
>
> The Lord has put away all your sins, and of your charity,
> pray for me, a sinner also.
> Amen.

4.3 Dynamic Scripture

Of course scripture is in itself dynamic – the stories, images and parables leap off the page and the teachings of Christ reach out to us across the millennia. But if that is the case, then why does the presentation of scripture in worship amount to the dull, monotonal recitation of some disjointed lines read badly through a third-rate PA system?

It would appear that the beauty and poetry of scripture are masked by a cloud of unpreparation, inattentiveness and a wholesale lack of creativity. We should therefore seek to try and inject into our presentation of scripture the passion and vividness of the original. We recall that scripture comes primarily from an oral tradition and that this implies a narrative beyond the simple written word. It would appear that the oral tradition dominated the transmission of the Good News for at least 30 years after the resurrection, before becoming crystallized into the written word. The oral tradition shapes and crafts a narrative, focuses on the key elements of a story and pulls from it the power to transfix, to enrapture, and, most significantly, to convert. This ultimately coalesces into a tradition which is not locked and static, but which is dynamic, for the retelling of a story will *always* require the involvement of the 'now', the present, to provide the context of the story. If we leave the narrative in aspic on the page, it is lifeless: the power of scripture is that it lies in the present.

The scriptures have the power to entertain. The Good Samaritan is possibly the most perfect story ever told: it features a contextual set-up (the scribe's question, 'Who is my neighbour?'), a scene set, a rounded three-part illustration, for two would just not be as clear, a question for all of us, scribe included, to answer ('Which of these three acted as a neighbour?') and a devastatingly powerful conclusion ('Go then and do likewise'). It speaks both to the scribe and directly to us as the third party hearing this narrative. In structure and style, it cannot be bettered.

Parables bring the Kingdom of God to life, but we must be aware that they were fresh expressions of their time: contextual, relevant and with the possibility of bringing the wonder of the Kingdom into mundane, impoverished lives. For these parables to regain their true power, we must consider the context of the hearers of today. At times, the context of the teaching remains unchanged, for God's truths remain eternal, and yet at times and for certain missional contexts, the same classic teachings need to be placed into a new environment.

It is therefore appropriate for a group of young people to draw from the Good Samaritan parable the tale of a man in the wrong kind of football shirt in the wrong part of town, whose 'Samaritan' turns out to be wearing the shirt of the old enemy.

This bloke was going through a rough part of town. It wasn't his town, and he didn't really belong here. You can think of your own local tensions: football teams, chav and grunge, colour of skin, there's no end of examples. Whatever it was, he was out on his own, in a vulnerable place, in the wrong place.

He got set upon, beaten, robbed and left in a bleeding, bruised pile on the pavement.

As our victim was lying there, he thought he could see someone coming down the street dressed in a dog collar – the local priest – he was saved! But the local priest had so much on his mind, Masses to say and masses to do, and he just looked past the man on the ground – a head so far in the clouds that he couldn't see the need in front of him.

A little while later, our victim lying there with bruised and swollen eyes thought he could see one of his own – the same football shirt, the same dress code, the same hairstyle or cap or whatever we choose to show our individuality with by being just like all our mates – he was saved! But his brother in fashion didn't want to get blood on him, didn't want to get involved, didn't want to put aside his plans for the day and deal with it – his life was already far too full to bother with this need.

When the victim thought that was it, that the end was near, there came another standing over him. Different. Different colour football shirt, different style of music coming over the iPod. Different. This means trouble, this means the end.

But the stranger, the man who had no ties to our victim, was the one to help him up, to get him to the hospital, to sort out the paperwork and the police, to help the victim get his life back together. He went out of his own way to make a difference to the victim, went the extra mile. Saw what was right.

Which of these three, asked Jesus, *was like a neighbour?*

The one who showed him kindness, he answered. Not the one whom everyone expects to be holy. Not the one who seemed to be from the same family, the same mindset, the same tribe. The one who looked beyond the badges and the labels and saw the need of another human being.

Jesus then gave those to whom he told this story a simple command:

Go then, and do likewise.

In no way does this undermine the parable, the teaching or the glory of what Jesus tells. In truth, I am convinced that if (and when) Jesus turns up to chat with my youth group, this is exactly how he would tell it.

The way in which scripture is presented is also open for exploration. In the past, chanting the text has beautified and glorified it: the Dominican chant of the prologue of John is a classical example, and the sung Passion on Good Friday continues to generate a huge emotional response. There are other ways of dramatizing the text.

The retelling of scripture should excite, challenge and even offend. A creative Mass was being celebrated at a fairly traditional and well-dressed church. The text was for All Saints' Day and featured the Beatitudes as the Gospel. With the connivance of the Incumbent, the intention was to restore to the Beatitudes some of the shock and offence that Jesus' countercultural message would have generated at the Sermon on the Mount. After a traditional and cosy beginning which saw a traditional Gospel line-up (servers and acolytes, a crucifer and a dignified procession into the midst of the congregation), we sought to blow that apart: departing from the set piece, the Beatitudes were declaimed from memory as we strode around the nave and confronted the congregation with these subversive truths face to face. (see 4.3.2, 'The Beatitudes in your face' below).

It was shocking. It was dramatic. It was, I am sure to many, offensive. That is *precisely* the point of that text, to confront the values of polite society with the values of the gospel. In the words of one commentator on the Ship-of-Fools discussion board:

> We had a Gospel procession like normal, but then instead of it being read plainly (and perhaps with dignity?) from the centre of the nave, the gospeller rather dramatically gave a reading while walking around the church in a rather invigorated/passionate manner. Which is all nice and good ... but once again it did somewhat shock the more conservative members of the congregation.[8]

Job done.

4.3.1 Two Gospels for the Price of One: John and Luke Remixed

Used at a Mass presided over by the Archbishop of Canterbury, we formed two traditional Gospel processions with all the pomp and circumstance associated with it: two crucifers, two thurifers, a pair of acolytes each. Each set off from a different edge and met before the principal celebrant, and then gave us this mélange especially for the Annunciation:

As two readers begin their Gospels, a foetus is shown on screen.
Audio: foetal heartbeat begins very low and rises in volume.

                                The Lord be with you.
                                And also with you.

The Lord be with you.
And also with you.

                                Hear the Gospel of our Lord Jesus
                                Christ according to Luke.
                                Glory to you, O Lord.

Hear the Gospel of our Lord Jesus
Christ according to John.
Glory to you, O Lord.

---

8 Reproduced with permission from the poster of the comment and the Ship of Fools <www.ship-of-fools.com> website.

In the sixth month the angel Gabriel was sent by God to a town in Galilee called Nazareth, to a virgin engaged to a man whose name was Joseph, of the house of David. The virgin's name was Mary.

In the beginning was the Word, and the Word was with God, and the Word was God. He was in the beginning with God.

And Gabriel came to Mary and said, 'Greetings, favoured one! The Lord is with you.' But she was much perplexed by his words and pondered what sort of greeting this might be. The angel said to her, 'Do not be afraid, Mary, for you have found favour with God.'

All things came into being through him, and without him not one thing came into being. What has come into being in him was life, and the life was the light of all people. The light shines in the darkness, and the darkness did not overcome it.

'And now, you will conceive in your womb and bear a son, and you will name him Jesus. He will be great, and will be called the Son of the Most High, and the Lord God will give to him the throne of his ancestor David. He will reign over the house of Jacob for ever, and of his kingdom there will be no end.'

There was a man sent from God, whose name was John. He came as a witness to testify to the light, so that all might believe through him. He himself was not the light, but he came to testify to the light.

Mary said to the angel, 'How can this be, since I am a virgin?' The angel said to her, 'The Holy Spirit will come upon you, and the power of the Most High will overshadow you; therefore the child to be born will be holy; he will be called Son of God.'

The true light, which enlightens everyone, was coming into the world. He was in the world, and the world came into being through him; yet the world did not know him. He came to what was his own, and his own people did not accept him.

'And now, your relative Elizabeth in her old age has also conceived a son; and this is the sixth month for her who was said to be barren. For nothing will be impossible with God.'

But to all who received him, who believed in his name, he gave power to become children of God, who were born, not of blood or of the will of the flesh or of the will of man, but of God.

Then Mary said, 'Here am I, the servant of the Lord; let it be with me according to your word.'

There is an almost imperceptible pause.

And the Word became flesh and lived among us, and we have seen his glory, the glory as of a father's only son, full of grace and truth.

The audio cuts out suddenly.

Together:

This is the Gospel of the Lord.
Praise to you, O Christ.

4.3.2 The Beatitudes in Your Face: Matthew 5.1–12

A traditional Gospel procession forms: crucifer, thurifer, acolytes. The gospeller prepares to deliver a traditional reading. After the introduction, he breaks from the servers and rounds on the congregation, delivering the Beatitudes in a confrontational style designed to upset and disturb. The Beatitudes should not be comfortable hearing, and it is right that they should disturb us.

The Lord be with you.
and also with you.

Hear the Gospel of Our Lord Jesus Christ, according to Matthew.
Glory to you, O Lord.

When Jesus saw the crowds, he went up on a hill and sat down. His followers came to him, and he began to teach them, saying:

The gospeller turns on the congregation, wandering among them and challenging them with the following text:

'They are blessed, those who realize their spiritual poverty,
  for the kingdom of heaven belongs to them.
They are blessed, those who grieve,
  for God will comfort them.
They are blessed, those who are humble,
  for the whole earth will be theirs.
They are blessed, those who hunger and thirst after justice,
  for they will be satisfied.
They are blessed, those who show mercy to others,
  for God will show mercy to them.
They are blessed, those whose thoughts are pure,
  for they will see God.
They are blessed, those who work for peace,
  for they will be called God's children.
They are blessed, those who are persecuted for doing good,
  for the kingdom of heaven belongs to them.'

'People will insult you and hurt you. They will lie and say all kinds of evil things about you because you follow me. But when they do, you will be blessed.
Rejoice and be glad, because you have a great reward waiting for you in heaven. People did the same evil things to the prophets who lived before you.'

The gospeller turns and returns to the sanctuary, almost spitting out the words:

This is the Gospel of the Lord.
Praise to you, O Christ.

4.3.3 Daybreak Responsory

Music: 'Time Passes', from the *Belly of an Architect* soundtrack.

The God of creation made the first day.
The sun rises and the sun sets.

Noah sat on the deck of his ark and watched a miracle.
The sun rises and the sun sets.

Joseph counted the days in his prison cell.
The sun rises and the sun sets.

David was inspired by the beauty of the sky.
The sun rises and the sun sets.

Mary prayed at sunset until morning when she could go to Jesus' tomb.
The sun rises and the sun sets.

We watch the days pass one by one.
The sun rises and the sun sets.

We enter into the night.
The sun rises and the sun sets.

God will keep us safe.
The sun rises and the sun sets.

God will give us rest.
The sun rises and the sun sets.

God will give us peace of mind.
Amen.

4.3.4 Washed Clean

There are times when words are not enough to convey the power of God. Some priests are drawn to illustrate this by fire-eating, juggling or illusions. This short homily uses some chemistry to illustrate these truths. You will need:

- Two clear glass bowls.
- 30mls of film fixer solution (which can still be bought from photographic shops, or over the internet).
- 10mls of iodine tincture (which can be bought from a pharmacy).
- A white handkerchief.
- Some water.

Prepare the bowls: one containing plain water and the other a diluted film fixer solution (which is not mentioned, let it remain a mystery). This text is aimed at children. You can express this shape in any way that fits your congregation.

Jesus Christ was a remarkable man: he said remarkable things, but even more remarkable were the things he did. I don't just mean amazing things like healing the sick, or even rising from the dead, although that is the most incredible thing that only the Son of God could do.

No, today I want to show you something quite special that illustrates what Jesus did for us, and continues to do for us as the Saviour of the world.

I have here, in these bowls, some water, as you can see: plain, ordinary water. Now these two bowls represent the world, and as the world is over 70 per cent water, it is quite right that they are full of water.

Now, here I have a handkerchief, a plain, ordinary handkerchief, and I think that it's even clean. This handkerchief represents us, people in the world; and as you can see, when I dip it into the clean water, it stays nice and bright and shiny.

However, the world isn't really as clean as all that, is it? There are lots of nasty things going on – people killing each other and hating each other, simply because they live in the wrong part of town, or because they have different colour skin; people arguing and stealing and telling lies, all things that make God very sad about the wonderful world that he created: failing to love God, failing to follow God's laws and failing to treat other people as we want to be treated.

So, to show this, I am going to add a few drops of some of this badness into the bowl of water, just a little, because I am sure that there is just a little bit of badness in the world; not a lot, but see what happens – the little bit of badness spreads throughout the earth and makes the water all mucky and brown.

See what happens when I dip the nice clean hankie into the water now.

(Put hankie in iodine solution, and it goes black.)

It makes it dirty and stained: we are affected by the badness in the world, and we are marked by it; see how the hankie goes black – and sometimes we even make the badness worse by adding our own badness: a bit of lying, a bit of cheating, a bit of stealing and a bit of failing to love God as we should. We call this turning away from God, 'sin'.

Now, in this other bowl, we have a slightly different world, a world which is touched with the love of Jesus Christ in it: he loves each and every one of us. No matter how discoloured and dirty we think we may be, no matter how clever we are or how we look, he simply loves us, no matter what

Watch what happens now, if I take the cloth that is us, marked with sin, and put it in the Jesus bowl ...

(Put cloth in fixer bowl, and it will turn 'clean' again as the fixer neutralizes the iodine.)

It takes away our sin, and makes us clean again, and you can see that the hankie has gone back to white again, as it has been touched by the love of Jesus.

However, and I think this is the clever part, this story does not end with our being wiped clean, and our being made clean of sin: watch what happens when I take the cloth that has encountered the love of Jesus, and put it back in the dirty, sinful old world again.

(Put the cloth from the fixer back in the iodine solution – the iodine will clear and the 'water' will be clean again.)

The love of Christ, which has changed you, has the power to change the world, and the effect of sin can be overcome.

Jesus Christ did this because he was the Messiah, the Son of God, as Peter had identified. The other readings we heard showed that as he turned this cloth back clean, so Jesus would make the world clean – what we call the Saviour of the world – he would bring good news to the oppressed, bind up the broken-hearted, proclaim liberty to the captives, and release to the prisoners; comfort all who mourn. Jesus did that by dying on the cross and by rising again to defeat death – defeating death for us all – that is why he really and truly is, 'the Saviour of the world'.

(Dispose of the water carefully, as the fixer solutions are poisonous.)

4.4 Eucharistic Prayers

It might be useful here to consider what makes a valid Eucharist. The Liturgical Commission in their *Common Worship* texts suggest that the least common denominator is the order described as 'A Service of the Word with Holy Communion'.

A Service of the Word with a Celebration of Holy Communion

This rite requires careful preparation by the president and other participants, and is not normally to be used as the regular Sunday or weekday service. Sections marked with an asterisk* must follow an authorized text.

Preparation

The people and the priest:

- greet each other in the Lord's name
- confess their sins and are assured of God's forgiveness*
- keep silence and pray a Collect.*

The Liturgy of the Word

The people and the priest:

- proclaim and respond to the word of God.

Prayers

The people and the priest:

- pray for the Church and the world.

The Liturgy of the Sacrament

The people and the priest:

- exchange the Peace
- prepare the table
- pray the Eucharistic Prayer*
- break the bread
- receive Holy Communion.

The Dismissal

The people and the priest:

• depart with God's blessing.

This structure is quite inappropriate as an authorization for creative Eucharist, as it insists on the use of authorized words of confession and the actual Eucharistic Prayer. There are times when it is necessary to exceed these boundaries. I have argued for the need for an Order Three in *Common Worship* which is entirely composed of rubric and places emphasis on the Anglican *shape* of the Eucharist while permitting a range of creativity within an authorized structure. To say that 'A Service of the Word' is an adequate provision for all creative liturgy dramatically understates the importance of creative or fresh liturgy in the growth of the Church, consigning it to a backwater of a half-forgotton liturgical oddity. It deserves its own Order if the Church is to value it properly.

Eucharistic prayers authorized by committee and then voted on in Synod must qualify as the least authoritative texts produced: a homogenization of all kinds of theologies, spiritualities and politicing which satisfies no one.

What is most important is the shape of the Eucharistic form, with words, images and rituals that are conducive to that shape, rather than the actual words used. The outline at the beginning of this chapter is a fuller version of that structure, but contains in detail a process which is characteristic of the *Common Worship* Order 1 without being tied down to it. If the idea of messing with the actual Eucharistic Prayer gives you anxiety, then I recommend sticking with Eucharistic Prayer B, the most complete and *proper* one.[9] The rest of it, including the preface of the prayer, is completely open to creative interpretation.

4.4.1 A Simple Mass

What happens when you need to celebrate the Eucharist simply and directly, with the minimum of fuss but with an atmosphere of mystery and expectation? This Eucharist grew from a quick service at the beginning of a youth all-night bowling event, and was mutated through Mass celebrated around a coffee table with a youth group. All it needs are a celebrating priest, two voices, bread and

---

9 You might want to look at the Church of South Africa Rite IV as an alternative. Eucharistic Prayers from sister churches in the Anglican Communion have a commended status and can be useful.

wine and a sense of mystery in the voice. Candles and incense burned in a balti dish can help.

Cel: God is here. Make yourselves at home.

1:       Come and stay a while, take a moment from your busy, hectic, Facebook-filled, MSN-clogged lives and pause.

2:       Wait for a moment and take the chance to sense he in whose presence we find ourselves.

Cel: Life is a like a journey, a long and sometimes lonely journey. This journey takes us from our comfortable and sometimes drab lives and into unfamiliar territory. It might be challenging, it might be hard. For any journey, we must be fed, prepared, sorted.

         In the name of the +Father and of the Son and of the Holy Spirit. Amen.

1:       Our preparation for this journey means sorting out our kit, getting it in order, and getting on the right track. There are many paths, and many of those paths might look attractive or easy, but they are not necessarily the right path.

2:       There are many paths with twists and turns, ups and downs, dead ends and frustrations, but only one true way.

1:       O Lord, for the many times that we have sought to take the easy path, Lord have mercy. **Lord have mercy**.

Cel: O Lord, for the distractions that have drawn us away from you, Christ have mercy. **Christ have mercy**.

2:       O Lord, for our lack of faith in you, and the direction you draw us to, Lord have mercy, **Lord have mercy**.

Cel: Almighty God, who loves you, walks with you, guides you and supports you through all the ups and downs of your life, and has given authority to his Church to absolve sins, free you from your burdens and + reconcile you to his heart. In the name of the man who was sent to save us. **Amen.**

Be fed, just as his first followers were fed in preparation for the journey ahead of them, a journey which would take a whole lifetime.

1:        St Paul said:

Let me go over with you again exactly what goes on in the Mass and why it is so centrally important. I received my instructions from the Man himself and passed them on to you. On the night of his betrayal, he took bread. Having given thanks, he broke it and said,

> 'This is my body, broken for you.
> Do this to remember me.'

After supper, he did the same thing with the cup:

> 'This cup is my blood, my new covenant with you.
> Each time you drink this cup, remember me.'

What you must solemnly realize is that every time you eat this bread and every time you drink this cup, you re-enact in your words and actions the death of the Man. You will be drawn back to this meal again and again until he returns.

(1 Corinthians 11.23–26)

2:        St John remembered:

The Man said: 'I am the bread of life; The living bread that comes down from heaven. If anyone eats of this bread, he will live for ever. And the bread that I will give for the life of the world is my flesh.'

'Whoever feeds on my flesh and drinks my blood has eternal life, and I will raise him up on the last day. For my flesh is true food, and my blood is true drink. Whoever feeds on my flesh and drinks my blood abides in me, and I in him.'

(John 6.48–56)

Cel: When his disciples, gathered in an upper room to eat a simple meal heard this, they had no idea what he meant: bread and wine become body and blood? How outrageous! It sounded a little like cannibalism – the Man who had guided them through so much, taught them so much, given them a glimpse of heaven on earth in wondrous signs and marvellous healings, was inviting them to eat of him.

And two thousand years later, he still sits among us, and invites us to his table. It doesn't matter where you've been, or what you've done, or how badly you think you have been in the past: the Man reaches out and offers you a place at this table, this place of encounter, this point of transformation.

The Lord be with you.
And also with you.

1: For he is with us, now. Supporting, guiding, counselling and comforting. Stirring up the complacent and crying out for justice, transforming lives and making whole.

Cel: Lift up your hearts.
We lift them up to the Lord.

2: The best way, the only way we can respond is in worship and in this sacred space drawing closer to God to the point where we can touch him, taste him and feel the difference.

Cel: Let us give thanks to the Lord our God.
It is right to give thanks and praise.

In ways which we do not understand, or could ever hope to understand, Christ is present in our midst. The many thousands, millions of words of theologians, the prayers of saints, the witness of the apostles: *none* of them have ever got their heads around what happens here.

1: We can't see the wind, but we know what happens to the trees.

2:         Look not for the wind, but for the effect of the wind.

1:         We can't see any outward change in bread and wine, but we know that something is different

2:         Look not for God hiding under an ordinary piece of bread, as St Francis once said, but look for the effect on those who share in the Body and Blood of Christ.

Cel: Bread: simple, wholesome, good. The staple of life and proof in our hands of God's bountiful goodness to us all.

Wine: source of joy and gladness, an example of God's love in a glistening drop of rich, dark sweetness.

Our prayers echo the song of the angels, saints, prophets and patriarchs and whole company of heaven as they say:

Holy, holy, holy Lord, God of power and might. Heaven and earth are full of your glory, Hosanna in the highest.

Blessed is he who comes in the name of the Lord. Hosanna in the highest.

Lord, you are holy indeed, the fountain of all holiness.
Let your Spirit come upon these gifts to make them holy,
so that they may become for us
the +body and blood of our Lord, Jesus Christ.
Before he was given up to death, a death he freely accepted,
he took bread and gave you thanks.
He broke the bread, gave it to his disciples, and said:

'Take this, all of you, and eat it:
this is my body which will be given up for you.'

When supper was ended, he took the cup.
Again he gave you thanks and praise, gave the cup to his disciples, and said:

'Take this, all of you, and drink from it:
this is the cup of my blood,
the blood of the new and everlasting covenant.
It will be shed for you and for all
so that sins may be forgiven.
Do this in memory of me.'

Together, let us remind ourselves of the mystery of faith:

Christ has died, Christ is risen, Christ will come again.

It's good.
It's changed.
And through it we are changed.

You won't find the Man
wedged between the crumbs,
but he is there.

He gives himself to us
in this way, so we can get our heads around the enormous idea of
God stepping down into our world.

He gives himself to us, so that we may become a part of him.

You eat food. It becomes a part of you.

You eat of this, and you become a part of him. A Holy Communion,
at one with God.

The only thing we can do is respond in love and joy, awe and
wonder.

May all of us who taste this foretaste of heaven be brought together
as your Church on this earth, empowered with the power of
God.

May we remember all those not with us, and bring us all into your
heavenly presence, through the powerful and mighty, saving work
of our Saviour.

Through him, with him, in him, in the unity of the Holy Spirit, all glory and honour is yours, almighty Father, for ever and ever. **Amen**.

I: He taught us to pray, so looking forward to when we can share this party again, let us pray:

Our Father, who art in heaven,
hallowed be thy name;
thy kingdom come;
thy will be done,
on earth as it is in heaven.
Give us this day our daily bread.
And forgive us our trespasses,
as we forgive those who trespass against us.
And lead us not into temptation;
but deliver us from evil.
For thine is the kingdom,
the power, and the glory,
for ever and ever.
Amen.

Come. Share. Eat at God's table.

I: No one is turned away.

2:   No one is unworthy.

Cel: All are welcome.

I: Take, break, share, and pass on.

2:   Be thankful. Be changed. Be aware that God is in our midst.

Distribution of Communion, usually passing it from one to another.

I: By this meal, we have been changed. By bread and wine transformed into the Body and Blood of Christ, you have been healed, restored, reinvigorated and renewed.

2:        You have been fed for life's journey with something more than a
         snack. You have been fed with the stuff of life.

Cel: The food of this earth just makes you hungry again. The food of this
         meal will last for ever. This bread and this wine are for all time.

         May your days be filled with laughter, joy and friendship.
         May your journey of life be guided by the Man.
         May your lives be transformed by this salvation story.
         And may the Blessing of God Almighty, +Father, Son and Holy
            Spirit,
         be upon you, and remain with you, this long night and always.
         Amen.

         The Mass has ended. Go in the peace of Christ.
         Thanks be to God.

4.4.2 Synchronized Eucharistic Prayers

The tradition of a musical underpinning of a Eucharistic prayer is nothing new:
organists have twiddled underneath the intonation of a priest for centuries; the
music can be improvised by a DJ or heavily rehearsed to a pre-defined video. In
order to get the timings correct, I add little markers to the video to ensure that
the image and words match. At the right are three dots which give 15 seconds of
warning, and the numbers refer to the section of the text.

Here is an example which can be integrated with a video from the DVD.
Sections 2 and 3 can fit almost every preface known in the Western Church.

For copyright reasons, the audio has been disabled on the DVD, but you might
like to set this video to 'Shine on you crazy diamond Part 1' by Pink Floyd, or see
the video on YouTube, <http://www.youtube.com/watch?v=H9FZpgdpYuA>.

1   The Lord be with you.
      And also with you.

      Lift up your hearts.
      We lift them to the Lord.

Let us give thanks to the Lord our God.
It is right to give thanks and praise.

2 Father, all-powerful and ever-living God,
we do well always and everywhere to give you thanks,
through Jesus Christ our Lord.

You renew the Church in every age by raising up men and women
outstanding in holiness, living witnesses of your unchanging love.
Saint Gregory brought us close to your mystery,
and taught us to love you as glorious Trinity: three in one.

3 We joyfully proclaim our faith in the mystery of your Godhead.
You have revealed your glory as the glory also of your Son
and of the Holy Spirit:
three Persons equal in majesty,
undivided in splendour,
yet one Lord, one God,
ever to be adored in your everlasting glory.

And so, with all the choirs of angels in heaven,
we proclaim your glory and join in their unending hymn of praise:

4 **Holy, holy, holy Lord,**
God of power and might,
heaven and earth are full of your glory.
Hosanna in the highest.
Blessed is he who comes in the name of the Lord.
Hosanna in the highest.

5 Lord, you are holy indeed, the source of all holiness;
grant that by the power of your Holy Spirit,
and according to your holy will,
these gifts of bread and wine
may be to us the +body and blood of our Lord Jesus Christ;

who, in the same night that he was betrayed,
took bread and gave you thanks;

he broke it and gave it to his disciples, saying:

6   Take, eat; this is my body which is given for you;
     do this in remembrance of me. +

7   In the same way, after supper
     he took the cup and gave you thanks;
     he gave it to them, saying:

     Drink this, all of you;
     this is my blood of the new covenant,
     which is shed for you and for many for the forgiveness of sins.
     Do this, as often as you drink it,
     in remembrance of me. +

8   Praise to you, Lord Jesus:

     **Dying, you destroyed our death,
     rising, you restored our life:
     Lord Jesus, come in glory.**

9   And so, Father, calling to mind his death on the cross,
     his perfect sacrifice made once for the sins of the whole world;
     rejoicing in his mighty resurrection and glorious ascension,
     and looking for his coming in glory,
     we celebrate this memorial of our redemption.

10   As we offer you this, our sacrifice of praise and thanksgiving,
     we bring before you this bread and this cup
     and we thank you for counting us worthy
     to stand in your presence and serve you.

11   Send the Holy Spirit on your people
     and gather into one in your kingdom
     all who share this one bread and one cup,
     so that we, in the company of Our Blessed Lady,

     (*insert your favourite saints and patrons here*)

and all the saints,
may praise and glorify you for ever,
through Jesus Christ our Lord;

12   by whom, and with whom, and in whom,
in the unity of the Holy Spirit,
all honour and glory be yours, almighty Father,
for ever and ever.
Amen.

(Preface: adapted from the Roman Prefaces of the Holy Men & Women and the Preface of the Holy Trinity; Eucharistic Prayer B from *Common Worship* © 2001 Archbishop's Council.)

4.4.3 Silent Eucharistic Prayer

'Preach the gospel', said St Francis of Assisi, 'using words only when you have to.'

Words	Actions
	Required: Loaf and bottle, corporal and corkscrew.
Lord, you are holy indeed, the source of all holiness; grant that by the power of your Holy Spirit, and according to your holy will, these gifts of bread and wine	Raise hands together upwards. Circle arms out wide.
may be to us the +body and blood of our Lord Jesus Christ;	Extend over elements.
who, in the same night that he was betrayed,	Grasp loaf and bottle and raise to chest height. Cross across chest

took bread and gave you thanks; he broke it and gave it to his disciples, saying:	Place down bottle. Pick up corporal, wrap loaf and cradle like a child.
Take, eat; this is my body which is given for you;	Unwrap. Break and hold wide in open arms gesture.
do this in remembrance of me.	Proffer to congregation and raise above head (bells).
In the same way, after supper he took the cup and gave you thanks;	Take bottle, and put in corkscrew, until arms are out in cross shape.
he gave it to them, saying: 'Drink this, all of you;	Make Benediction blessing.
this is my blood of the new covenant, which is shed for you and for many for the forgiveness of sins.	Remove cork and pour from great height into chalice.
Do this, as often as you drink it, in remembrance of me.'	Proffer to congregation and raise above head (bells).

Some communities might prefer to show the words of the Eucharistic prayer behind the celebrant as he/she offers the sacrifice. I tend to mutter the words of the prayer *sotto voce* as I mime them, not only to ensure they are complete, but also to ensure that it remains valid and to placate those who might find this a step too far.

(Eucharistic Prayer B from *Common Worship* © 2001 Archbishop's Council.)

4.4.4 Prefaces for Different Occasions

The *Common Worship* Prefaces to the Eucharistic Prayers are indeed worthy, but they do not always speak to the need at hand. At times, other Prefaces taken from other Churches and traditions might suit. The Roman Missal has a number of very effective Prefaces which can be combined with a different Eucharistic prayer, or it might just be appropriate to create a new Preface afresh.

Prefaces begin with an address to the Father, with reference to the Son, and conclude with a recognition that we pray alongside the company of heaven, which leads us effectively to the *Sanctus*. What happens in between is largely a matter of the case in hand.

Many of these Prefaces can be illustrated by image or video, or accompanied by music, as deemed appropriate.

4.4.4.1 Mass of the Edge

Celebrated in the midst of a group of broken people in broken times. These words (which came from them and through them) spoke of the reality of their pain, resolution through the cross and looking for healing and redemption.

Father, all-powerful and everliving God,
We bring to this table all that is painful in our lives.

Our disappointments,
our failures,
our addictions,
ourselves.

In that bringing we come to the foot of your cross,
where you raise all of this up
and our pain is overshadowed by your victory
over sin and death,
over pain and suffering,
over abuse and addiction.

So that we may join our prayers with the redeemed and renewed
company of heaven, forever praising you and saying:

Holy, Holy, Holy Lord ...

4.4.4.2 Mass of Unity

Father, almighty and ever-living God,
we do well always and everywhere to give you thanks,
through Jesus Christ, your only Son, our Lord.

By the redeeming work of love,
by the pouring out upon the cross,
by the power of the resurrection,
and the enthusing of the Holy Spirit.

We are united as one body, one heart, one mind,
and are enfolded in the love of God
through Christ, our redeemer and brother.

Therefore with angels and animals,
microbes and mountains,
and all that lives for you,
we proclaim how wonderful you are.
We pour out our thanks to you
in a song that never sleeps:

Holy, Holy, Holy Lord …

4.4.5 Different Locations, Different Positions

If, as we have established, we hold all of life to be sacramental, then the sacraments can and should be celebrated in places and locations outside of the church building: on the grass, at a building site of a new project, on a coffee table surrounded by the faithful. I am reminded of the words of Dom Gregory Dix: 'He told His friends to do this henceforth with the new meaning "for the *anamnesis* of Him", and they have always done it since.'

Was ever another command so obeyed? For century after century, spreading slowly to every continent and country and among every race on earth, this action has been done, in every conceivable human circumstance, for every conceivable human need from infancy and before it to extreme old age and after it, from the pinnacles of earthly greatness to the refuge of fugitives in the caves and dens of the earth. Men have found no better thing than this to do for kings at their crowning and for criminals going to the scaffold; for armies in triumph or for a bride and groom in a little country church; for the proclamation of a dogma or for a good crop of wheat; for the wisdom of the parliament of a mighty nation or for a sick old woman afraid to die; for a schoolboy sitting an examination or for Columbus setting out to discover America; for the famine of whole provinces or for the soul of a dead lover; because the Turk was at the gates of Vienna; for the repentance of a soul; for the settlement of a strike; for a son for a barren woman; while the lions roared in the nearby amphitheatre; on the beach at Dunkirk; while the hiss of scythes in the thick June grass came faintly through the windows of a church; tremulously, by an old monk on the fiftieth anniversary of his vows; furtively, by an exiled bishop who had hewn timber all day in a prison camp near Murmansk; gorgeously, for the canonization of St Joan of Arc – one could fill many pages with the reasons why men have done this, and not tell a hundredth part of them. And best of all, day by day, week by week, month by month, on a hundred thousand successive Sundays, faithfully, unfailingly, across all the parishes of Christendom, the presbyters have done this just to make the *plebs sancta Dei* – the holy common people of God.[10]

Dom Gregory Dix OSB

When set out like this, it becomes clear that God cannot be limited to consecrated space, for indeed as the creator of the whole universe, there is nowhere that the Lord may not be found.[11] If we are to reclaim this world for Christ, then our Eucharistic actions begin this process and act as witness.

4.4.6 Mass of Revelation

Candlemas is all about the revelation of God in Christ. At the Presentation in the Temple, Jesus is a little further revealed; so for this Mass of Candlemas, we tried to explore this in new and creative ways.

Voile is a wonderful tool in creative worship because it is both a cheap and beautiful cloth available in many (liturgical) colours. It can be used to wrap beautiful objects, and conceal ugly ones, it can be lit underneath by fairy lights, and, because of its translucency, it can be projected onto from both sides. During

---

10 G. Dix (2005), *The Shape of the Liturgy*. London: Continuum.
11 Psalm 139: 'If I go up the mountain you are there, if I go to the depths of the earth, you are there.'

this Eucharistic preface, a large piece of voile was draped over the celebrant, the low altar and the congregation. During the Preface, the voile was slowly lifted so that, by the end of the *Sanctus*, the Eucharist, with Jesus present on the altar, is fully revealed.

> Father we begin buried, hemmed in, subjucated and hidden. Our faith covered by our sin, hidden by our insecurity.
>
> Yet you have revealed your love for us, uncovering yourself through the enfleshment of your Son, and continue to work through the power of your Holy Spirit.
>
> Reveal yourself to us in bread and wine,
> make us complete by the obedience of your Son to death, even death on a
>   cross.
> Take us and fashion us,
> form us in love into the likeness of Christ,
> and enable us to be freed to see that likeness in others.
>
> So we enter into the mysteries of heaven echoing the song of the angels, saints, prophets and patriarchs:
>
> Holy, Holy, Holy …

4.5 Intercessions

Prayer is an integral part of the Eucharistic celebration, and is one of the spheres of worship most open to creative innovation. It can take many forms.

4.5.1 Written Intercessions

This is a simple form of intercession, requiring just strips of paper and pens. You can then link each strip into a chain which you can wind around the altar at the offertory.

The people write their intercessions on the strips of paper.

If you want to write down your prayers, what would it look like?
A shopping list?
Would it be more like a doodle?
Would your prayers form a little sketch?
A spider diagram?
A single word?
Logical in structure? Random or chaotic?
Does it matter?
Before you write anything down, pause and reflect.
What is your main concern?
What do you need to bring before God?
For yourself.
For others.
For the Church.
For the world.
For the sick, the ailing, the addicted, the troublesome.
For the dead and the mourning.
We do not pray alone.
We join these prayers with all the others written tonight.
Woven together. Linked. Joined.
Joined with the angels, the saints, the prophets, the patriarchs.
Joined with the prayers of our Blessed Lady.

Hail Mary, full of grace,
the Lord is with thee.
Blessed art thou among women,
and blessed is the fruit
of thy womb, Jesus.
Holy Mary, Mother of God,
pray for us sinners now,
and at the hour of our death.

How did they turn out?
No need to sign your prayers.
God knows.
He knows your needs,
your desires,

your concerns ...

... and he listens.

He responds.

Whether you prayed a picture, a list, a diagram, a single word –

God responds.

Maybe yes,

maybe no,

maybe not yet.

Not always the answer to your prayers that you want –

but he answers.

Always.

Amen.

(Caroline Rhodes[12])

4.5.2 Visual Intercessions

Anglicans are especially inculturated to the written word: it's all about prayer books and hymnals, and yet, while it might have been right for Thomas Cranmer, it isn't the preferred method of encountering God for everyone. Visual Intercessions have therefore been a way of redressing the balance for those of us who pray with images better than with words. I know that many people will find this form of prayer unconventional or uncomfortable, but for some it will give far greater opportunities for prayer.

At its most basic level, you can pray creatively with a bunch of photographs or even images cut out from newspapers and stuck on to card, handed round a small group and contemplated on. It might be a series of ikons or religious paintings from the Classical era, or more modern images. A good place for these can be websites such as Artcyclopedia <www.artcyclopedia.com> which is an index of classical and modern themes and links you to the websites of galleries around the world.

You can draw from the website of news services such as the BBC (although the images are often small) or Reuters or simply take the risk and dive into Google Images – an index of all images on the internet. You will soon realize that the quality and appropriateness of the image you find is directly proportional to the

12 With permission from the author.

care with which you phrase the search term. Search in lots of different ways so you can choose the most appropriate with care. The first image you find is probably not the best one.

When you search for an image, you will find size and scale information in the Google search page. This should be taken note of, because most images are optimized for use on web pages, not the screen or the printer. When small images are blown up to full page size or printed out, they may appear 'blocky' or of very poor quality. If this is the case, move on to the next image. You often find that the same image can appear a number of times but in different qualities, and a little more searching can reveal the perfect image for your need.

These electronic images may be used in a number of different ways: in a slideshow on a laptop as a part of an Installation, or loaded into a digital photo frame. Care needs to be exercised to crop or resize the image so that the aspect ratio (the relative height and width of the image) does not result in a distorted image. A careful crop or zoom might make all the difference.

The simplest visual intercession for a large group is the display of the images through PowerPoint accompanied by a selected piece of music. Control of the images is done by an operator and works best with reflective, softer images for a more meditative tone. The music may be embedded in the first slide, or played externally on a CD player.

More complex visual intercessions can be created by making them into a video. See section 3.4 on video creation. The advantage of a video is that, once created, it is entirely standalone, containing image and music perfectly synchronized.

Not everyone responds to visual intercessions – some auditory learners have problems with them – but many more people are visual learners, and they allow them to explore intercessory prayer in a creative response, as an image will guide two different people to have different foci of prayer.

4.6 Stations and Labyrinths

Alternative worship simply loves Stations. The idea of moving to a place in a form of mini-pilgrimage is ancient: the Stations of the Cross is a devotion in your own church specifically for those unable to make the pilgrimage to Jerusalem to walk the Via Dolorosa itself.

4.6.1 Via Dolorosa: A Complete Multimedia Stations of the Cross

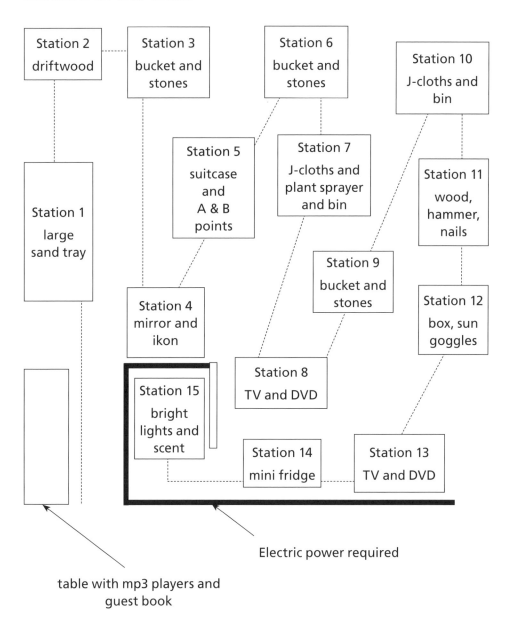

Station 2 driftwood

Station 3 bucket and stones

Station 6 bucket and stones

Station 10 J-cloths and bin

Station 5 suitcase and A & B points

Station 7 J-cloths and plant sprayer and bin

Station 11 wood, hammer, nails

Station 1 large sand tray

Station 9 bucket and stones

Station 12 box, sun goggles

Station 4 mirror and ikon

Station 15 bright lights and scent

Station 8 TV and DVD

Station 13 TV and DVD

Station 14 mini fridge

Electric power required

table with mp3 players and guest book

4.6.1.1 Set up and Installation

This should help you set up and create these multimedia stations.

Kit List

This is what I think you need.

- **MP3 or CD players**. The Stations work best when done individually. The files can be burnt to a CD or copied onto MP3 players. You only need the small, cheap and basic 128Mb MP3 players. MP3 is better than CD as CDs can sometimes skip or jump. You will need **people** on hand to hand out and receive back the players.

- **Large sandbox or tarpaulin and quite a lot of sand**. We created a 12ft by 8ft wooden box, but a tarpaulin that size should be able to contain the sand, which needs to be deep enough to walk through. We used 16 large bags of play sand in that tray.

- **A large piece of rough wood**. We found some driftwood on the beach; or some other big heavy piece of timber would work well to give the impression of the cross. Splinters are good. Forget the anxieties about health and safety: good religion is *dangerous*.[13]

- **Three large buckets and a large number of palm-sized stones** which can be got from a garden centre or from the beach.

- **Large mirror and ikon of the Pantocrator** (see right) arranged so that you can see both the ikon and your own reflection in the mirror.

- **A large suitcase with something heavy in it**. It's good to find a use for those old hymn books!

- **Two rolls of J-cloths**, a **plant sprayer** (to make the cloths moist on one Station) and **two small bins** to dispose of them.

- **Two TVs and DVD players**. The video loops are designed to play continuously on a standard DVD player.

- **A large block of wood, a claw hammer and some 6-inch nails.**

---

13 Matthew 24.7–14.

- **Sunbed or welding goggles** that are as dark as possible.

- A **large box, perhaps with some black cloth** on the front to create as dark and claustrophobic space as possible.

- **A mini-fridge** (or a normal-sized fridge).

- **Bright lights** (spotlights or the arc-lamps you can get from a DIY store) and an **aromatherapy-scent plugin room freshener.**

- **Gaffer tape** – not only does it hold the universe together, but it can be used to mark the path on the floor. As you can see from our plan, we did not make a geometrical shape, wanting to move away from the idea that this was a labyrinth. In *Blesséd*'s view, although God is filled with order and beauty, our lives tend to be much messier.

If you want to create a proper labyrinth-style geometrical pattern, then feel free to do so <http://web.ukonline.co.uk/paradigm/discoverframe.html> is a good starting place for the design.

Guest Book is useful to gather comments after the Stations. People should be warned that it takes about an hour to do the Stations and that they should follow each track with a Station. There is one track before, as you travel to the first Station, and one track at the end as you return to the desk.

The layout is merely what we created at Walsingham. You should be prepared to adapt and modify the Stations for your needs; as long as they suit the recordings, you can be as creative as possible to achieve what you want to achieve.

Introduction

Audio: Massive Attack: 'Teardrop'.
Opening sign: prepare for journey.

We are going on a journey … but we do not make it alone.

Nearly 2,000 years ago, one Man walked a lonely path, and for centuries pilgrims have walked in his footsteps.

From across the known world they endured the hardships of pilgrimage before they even got to Jerusalem. Once there, they walked the Via Dolorosa – the way of sorrows – to see what the Man suffered, to reflect on what he saw, to consider his gift to us all.

Not all of us have the privilege to travel to Jerusalem, even in this age of jet travel, and so we bring that way of sorrows to us; and for us, this will be our pilgrimage today.

As we journey past each of these 15 Stations, we do not merely hark back to a journey made long ago, but we bring this journey into our journey, his presence into our present. We have the opportunity to walk beside him, and he has the opportunity to walk beside us as we cast aside our twenty-first-century cares and preoccupations on the roadway.

Take time, use space, explore your senses as they explore the Via Dolorosa: a way of sorrows, a way of meaning, a way of truth, a way of life.

1. Condemned

Station: sand on large tray.
Audio: Labyrinth: 'Letting Go' (instrumental).
Sign: Jesus is condemned.

It can sometimes be a lonely road we travel down. At one point it seems that we are buoyed on by the crowd, carried along to a destination not of our choosing, not caring to where we are led, and then we are left alone: stranded, isolated.

There is a well-known story of a man who walks along a beach, and he glances over his shoulder and sees that in addition to his own footprints in the sand, there is another set of footprints walking beside him. He realizes that this walk on the beach is a symbol of his life and that the footprints beside him are those of God, walking with him, each step of the way.

As he looks closer, he sees that at some times in his life, there is only one set of footprints; and he recognizes those phases in his life as the times that were difficult and challenging. He turns to God and says, 'Why did you desert me in those difficult times in my life. Why did you leave me alone?'

'Ah,' says God. 'Those difficult times in your life, and the single set of footprints – those are the times when I carried you.'

Take off your shoes. Take off your socks. Take off your shoes. Take off your socks.

Walk the sand, be conscious of the presence of God beside you. Let no one else distract you, for you begin your journey across this sand. Walk back and forth if you need.

Walk the sand. They say that a journey of a thousand miles begins with a single step.

Walk the sand. Walk the lonely road.

Walk the sand. Consider the times when you felt isolated and alone, condemned.

Walk the sand. Feel it on your feet. Walking the sand is harder than walking on grass, more effort than walking the streets. Make the effort and walk on. Walk the sand.

The Man began the journey down the Via Dolorosa, the way of sorrows, in a crowd, but isolated and alone: condemned by the crowd and by Pilate – a man too weak to resist the baying of the mob.

The Man walked this road, as you do now. When the crowd pressed in on him and threw false accusations at him, it may have felt as though he was on his own.

There was only one set of prints in the sand. The Man did not walk alone, but was carried. You do not walk alone. You walk with God.

There is no condemnation. The Man carries that for you. Walk on. Walk the sand.

Sotto voce:
Our Father, who art in heaven,
hallowed be thy name;
thy kingdom come;
thy will be done,
on earth as it is in heaven.
Give us this day our daily bread.
And forgive us our trespasses,
as we forgive those who trespass against us.
And lead us not into temptation;
but deliver us from evil. Amen.

2. Cross

Station: piece of rough, damp wood. Feel, sense, smell, put cheek on wood.
Audio: Nitin Sawhney: 'Spark' from Philtre *(instrumental).*
Sign: Jesus receives his cross.

'Pick up your cross daily and follow me.'

The Man has made it real for you. Feel the reality of the wood. Run your hand around it. Smell it.

Place your cheek against the wood that would be for the Man his earthly destiny – just as he predicted.

Feel the weight. Feel the roughness. Feel the reality of the wood. Place your cheek against it.

This is not a precious object made of gold or silver, stuck a long way away on an altar somewhere, processed around with triumph and dignity; not an intricate piece of jewellery placed around the neck of a loved one because it is pretty or a fashion statement.

It is part of a killing machine. An 8-feet-high dangerous killing-machine. It is visceral. It is real.

The Man had to carry one like this. Heavier. Rougher. He had to carry his cross when weighed down by exhaustion and a vicious beating.

Feel the weight. Feel the roughness. Feel the reality of the wood.

Smell the wood and imagine on it the smell of sweat and of blood: the smell of death which penetrates into the porous, living wood.

When the Man picked up his cross, he also picked up those burdens that we have: our concerns, our worries, our preoccupations, our real lives.

Feel the weight. Feel the roughness. Feel the reality of the wood.

This is real. Our lives are real, our burdens are real, visceral, heavy and sometimes painful. Work, college, exams, family life and relationships: the pain of togetherness and the bitterness of separatedness. All of these we must carry.

Our hope, our joy, our frustrations are inherent in the carrying of this cross. Ask yourself what burdens you are carrying, whose guilt, which problems, and give them over to the Man, who will willingly carry them for you.

Sotto voce:
Our Father, who art in heaven,
hallowed be thy name;
thy kingdom come;
thy will be done,
on earth as it is in heaven.
Give us this day our daily bread.
And forgive us our trespasses,
as we forgive those who trespass against us.
And lead us not into temptation;
but deliver us from evil. Amen.

3. Falls

Station: stone into bucket.
Audio: David Bowie: 'Moss Garden'.
Sign: Jesus falls for the first time.

Take some slow, deep breaths. Slow your breathing and clear your thoughts.

In front of you are a pile of stones and a pool of water. Take a stone from the pile. Imagine that all of your concerns and worries are held in the stone.

Hold the stone quietly and name the concerns and worries in your mind. Hold the stone over the pool of water. In your own time let it go. Watch your concerns and worries fall.

Imagine them falling into God's lap. How does it feel to release it?

The weight of the cross made the Man stumble. Down on his knees. The heavy, wooden killing-machine forcing him to the ground. Out of humiliation comes triumph, each stumble is not giving in to sin or failure, but is an overcoming of it: we must be prepared to pick ourselves up and carry on. Persevering after a fall is glory.

We carry our burdens, worries, cares with us; and we too will fall, overladen with grief, unbalanced by concern.

What have you to let fall? What have you to let the Man take from you?

Sotto voce:
Glory be to the Father,
and to the Son,
and to the Holy Spirit.
As it was in the beginning,
is now, and ever shall be,
world without end. Amen.

4. Mother

Station: mirror with image of Jesus placed at angles, so you can see your face and Jesus' face at the same time.
Audio: Moonwatcher: 'Sofa Loafer'.
Sign: Jesus meets his Mother.

Look. Look upon his face. You see a face which has been beaten, which is exhausted, which is weighed down by a final journey.

Look upon your own face. Look at your eyes. Are they exhausted? Are they weighed down? Can you see in your face things which concern or preoccupy you?

Look not for the signs of age, or for hints of imperfection; for you are wonderfully made, and whether four, or fourteen, or forty, you are made in God's image. To see oneself, or to see others, is to see the miracle of creation, the glory of God in each and every person. In every freckle, in every wrinkle, in every spot or every hair.

The Man encountered the person who loved him most on this earth – his first apostle, the bearer of his good news: a woman who had known the trials and tribulations of persecution, of being a refugee, of joy and miracles, and now seeing her own pushed to the point of death.

Look. Look upon his face and see the cares of the world. Can you see the cares of the world in your image as well?

The Man's mother looked upon this face, and felt the sword piercing her heart in compassion and love. She looks also upon your face, sees the tired eyes and the wry smile, she sees beyond the mask you wear for the day; and she understands.

Imagine what she goes through.

Put yourself in his place and see the compassionate gaze of the Man's mother reflecting back at you.

What words would you give in this encounter? What would you say to the person who loved you the most if you met them on the Via Dolorosa. Words of encouragement? Words of apology? Words. Or would the eyes say it all?

Look. Look upon his face.

Look. Look upon your own face.

Sotto voce:
Hail Mary, full of grace, the Lord is with thee.
Blessed art thou among women, and blessed is the fruit of thy womb, Jesus.
Holy Mary, Mother of God,
pray for us sinners now, and at the hour of our death.

5. Simon

Station: lift something heavy, like a suitcase. Two points marked on ground: A & B.
Audio: Luminus; 'Hold On'.
Sign: Simon helps Jesus carry his cross.

Jesus offered to share our burdens with us, he did so willingly. But Simon was coerced into it. At the point of the sword, he was commanded to share the burden, to bear the load.

Before you is a burden. It has travelled a long way, and yet is still far from its destination. You could be asked to carry it, and out of the goodness of your heart, out of your willingness to help others, you may wish to willingly move it from one place to another.

Please will you help me move this load? Can you assist me to get it from point A to point B?

It is heavy. It may be too heavy for you. You might consider it a trifle, a show of your strength and a tribute to your hardness. Or your dedication. Or your faith.

But what if I commanded you? What if I ordered you? What if I put a knife to your throat, a gun to your back and *made* you do it. You MUST move this from B to A. Do it! Do it now! Now!

Do you feel the prickle of resentment? Do you feel the humiliation? The sense of powerlessness? Do you hate me for it?

Do you resent the person who wasn't able to carry it in the first place? It's theirs after all, not yours; it's their problem, their death, their execution, just let me be and let them get on with it.

But your life is at risk. Move it. Move it from A to B. Move it now. I don't care if it's a struggle, but move it. Do it!

Please. Please can you move it from B to A. Could you help me?

Oh, you're too kind.

Thank you.

Our Father, who art in heaven,
hallowed be thy name;
thy kingdom come;
thy will be done,
on earth as it is in heaven.
Give us this day our daily bread.
And forgive us our trespasses,
as we forgive those who trespass against us.
And lead us not into temptation;
but deliver us from evil. Amen.

6. Falls

Station: stone into bucket.
Audio: David Bowie: 'Moss Garden'.
Sign: Jesus falls for the second time.

Take some slow, deep breaths. Slow your breathing and clear your thoughts.

In front of you are a pile of stones and a pool of water. Take a stone from the pile. Imagine that all of your concerns and worries are held in the stone.

Hold the stone quietly and name the concerns and worries in your mind. Hold the stone over the pool of water. In your own time let it go. Watch your concerns and worries fall.

Imagine them falling into God's lap. How does it feel to release it?

Haven't we been here before? Didn't the Man fall earlier? Didn't you do the same thing with the stone before?

If we were able to let go at our first attempt, then many things in this life would be easier than they really are. If we were able to truly turn from our misdeeds, to repent of our sinfulness, then we could really move on down this way of sorrows.

The Man fell once more. Beaten, exhausted. Lower, more desperate.

We fall repeatedly, we turn from God almost as often as we turn to him, and yet he is still there when we pick ourselves up once more. No matter how often we fall, we can be reconciled. Turn the stone again, lose your fears and inhibitions, leave your cares and worries and let God be there for you. There is the glory of God to be found in your struggles. Not humiliation or shame, but the shining glory of God reflected in a ripple of water.

Again.

And again.

Sotto voce:
Glory be to the Father,
and to the Son,
and to the Holy Spirit.

As it was in the beginning,
is now, and ever shall be,
world without end. Amen.

7. Veronica

Station: damp cloth onto face.
Audio: Proost: 'Holy Space' (Labyrinth instrumental).
Sign: Veronica offers Jesus a towel.

Amid the chaos of the baying crowd, amid the taunts, the spitting, the revulsion of a crowd that five days earlier had been praising God for the Man, a woman pushes through to the front and steps out into the path of the Condemned One.

Whereas everyone else is offering taunts and threats, she offers to wipe the face of the Man.

A cooling towel. A moment's release.

Take a towel from the pile. Place it over your own face. Feel the coolness and dampness.

Let it refresh you. Let it rest on your face. Let it refresh you from whatever makes you uncomfortable. Feel the cool refreshment of water on your face. Whatever makes you feel dirty, whatever weighs you down, whatever from which you seek to be cleansed.

Like an oasis of coolness, the Man was given a moment of relief, a brief pause. You could be the receiver of this grace, or you could be the giver.

It could be you offering a crumb of comfort, a kindly word, a brief moment of respite.

It could be you offering the towel.

Our Father, who art in heaven,
hallowed be thy name;
thy kingdom come;
thy will be done,
on earth as it is in heaven.
Give us this day our daily bread.

And forgive us our trespasses,
as we forgive those who trespass against us.
And lead us not into temptation;
but deliver us from evil. Amen.

(*Kindly dispose of your towel in the nearby bin. Thank you.*)

8. Women

Station: video/DVD: image loop of the Holocaust.
Audio: Oxford Camerata: 'Lamentations for Five Voices'. Composed by Robert
White (1538–1574).
Sign: Jesus meets the women of Jerusalem.

Watch.

Do you see these images of degradation, of holocaust, of genocide?

Do you sit passively and let them float over you?

Do you make a token response? Does it touch you because you feel it *ought*
to touch you?

Do you see these as images? Do you see them as real people? What if you
were confronted by this camp, this horror, this challenge? What if you were
here in real life? Would it touch you differently?

On his journey down the Via Dolorosa, the way of sorrows, the Man passed
a group of women. They mourned and wailed, they gave voice to the injustice
and inequity of their times, and of all time. They cried the cry of women the
world over who are oppressed and abused and disregarded by society, by
the Church, and by those whose role should be to protect them and their
children.

The Man said, 'Weep not for me.'

(*Echos: weep not for me, weep not for me, for me, for me, me, me.*)

The Man said, 'Weep for yourselves and your children.' We see what these
women and their daughters would have to weep over. We see, but do we
engage?

We watch, but do we feel the need to act?

You may be able to think of places and situations in the world which cry out for justice, for the intervention of God, for some miraculous *Deus Ex Machina* to descend from the clouds and to stop the war, the hunger, the poverty. We pray for God to dig us out of the holes of our own making, to clean up the mess we have made of our world, to put the bandage on the wounds of our inhumanity and to make it better.

We might hope that God will ride in on a white charger and save the world, remove our oppressors and rebalance our injustices; but these are our tasks. To make *thy kingdom come* we need to deal with these injustices, we need to right our own wrongs and make things ready for the Man's return. We have so much spring-cleaning to do, in both our own world and in our own lives. Until then, there is so much to weep over. Yes, weep now, then deal with it, and ensure that the tears of the world are dried.

Sotto voce:
Hail Mary, full of grace, the Lord is with thee.
Blessed art thou among women, and blessed is the fruit of thy womb, Jesus.
Holy Mary, Mother of God,
pray for us sinners now, and at the hour of our death.

9. Falls

Station: stone into bucket.
Audio: David Bowie: 'Moss Garden'.
Sign: Jesus falls for the third time.

Take some slow, deep breaths. Slow your breathing and clear your thoughts.

In front of you are a pile of stones and a pool of water. Take a stone from the pile. Imagine that all of your concerns and worries are held in the stone.

Hold the stone quietly and name the concerns and worries in your mind. Hold the stone over the pool of water. In your own time let it go. Watch your concerns and worries fall.

Imagine them falling into God's lap. How does it feel to release it?

Did you just throw the stone in without being told what to do? Did you just do it out of habit? Was it instinctive, intuitive? Did knowing what you were supposed to do stop you thinking about it?

Yes, we fall. Again and again, just as the Man fell for the third time. Does knowing that make it easier? Does it make you glib about your falling short?

Sotto voce:
Glory be to the Father,
and to the Son,
and to the Holy Spirit.
As it was in the beginning,
is now, and ever shall be,
world without end. Amen.

10. Stripped

Station: pieces of J-cloth to be ripped.
Audio: David Bowie: 'Ian Fish UK Heir'.
Sign: Jesus is stripped of his clothes.

Your clothes say so much about you. You may be a fashion junkie, you may not care at all about your appearance. Either way, it is a statement. Even by choosing not to, you are defined by your clothes: your culture, your faith, your work, your social status are all signified by what hides your nakedness.

Adam and Eve hid themselves in shame rather than appear naked. They began to use their outward selves to hide their inner beings. Vulnerable. Reduced. Shamed.

At the foot of the cross, the Man is reduced to such nakedness. The blood and sweat-stained clothes are not carefully removed, but torn from his back.

Vulnerable. Reduced. Shamed.

Take a cloth from the pile. Rip it. Tear it from the back of the Man. Feel the cloth give way under your power.

Vulnerable. Reduced. Shamed.

They ripped the cloth from his back, and divided it among themselves, leaving a Man about to die with nothing. Only his undershirt remained, the last thing of his and the only thing worth anything. Too good to rip apart, they threw dice for it.

Recall your most embarrassing moments. The times when you wanted the earth to open up and swallow you, when you felt at your weakest and most vulnerable. Was it like this?

Vulnerable. Reduced. Shamed. Was it at all like this? What would you think of those who inflicted this upon you? Would you hate them? Would you feel loathing, or would you not be able to raise your gaze from the ground, so great was your humiliation?

You are left with a pile of rags in tatters. Is this your dignity too? In tatters? The Man took his humiliation, and bears yours also. He stands before his tormentors as naked as the day he was laid in the animal trough. But out of this humiliation comes another triumph.

Our Father, who art in heaven,
hallowed be thy name;
thy kingdom come;
thy will be done,
on earth as it is in heaven.
Give us this day our daily bread.
And forgive us our trespasses,
as we forgive those who trespass against us.
And lead us not into temptation;
but deliver us from evil. Amen.

(*Kindly dispose of your cloth in the nearby bin. Thank you.*)

11. Nailed

Station: hammer a big nail into wood.
Audio: David Bowie: 'Subterranians'.
Sign: Jesus is nailed to the cross.

'Father, forgive them, for they know not what they do.'

Pick up one of the nails.

'Father, forgive them, for they know not what they do.'

Big. Hard. Nasty. Unforgiving.

'Father, forgive them, for they know not what they do.'

There is no yield in these skewers. Nowhere to run from. No way to escape the awful reality of what you about to do.

'Father, forgive them, for they know not what they do.'

Pick up that hammer. Feel its weight. It bears the weight of your life and your actions in a pound of heavy steel. It weighs heavy your preoccupations.

'Father, forgive them, for they know not what they do.'

Drive a nail into the wood. Go on. Do it. Imagine that it's not the bare wood you are nailing but there is actual flesh, real, live, warm flesh between your cold, hard nail and the dead wood. You can feel its warmth against your skin. It gives a little as you put the sharp point up against it, and you drive the nail home.

'Father, forgive them, for they know not what they do.'

… is what the Man says – amid the pain, the blood, the sweat, the anguish. He cries out:

'Father, forgive them, for they know not what they do.'

Do you know what you do? Are you aware of each little nail, each little hurtful remark or harmful glance that you drive into others, into those around you, into those you love?

The Man knows and feels. Each hammer-blow piercing his flesh. He feels what you inflict. On him, and on others. And yet still:

'Father, forgive them, for they know not what they do.'

Do you know what you do?

Our Father, who art in heaven,
hallowed be thy name;
thy kingdom come;
thy will be done,
on earth as it is in heaven.
Give us this day our daily bread.
And forgive us our trespasses,
as we forgive those who trespass against us.
And lead us not into temptation;
but deliver us from evil. Amen.

12. Dies

Station: look into a box that is unremittingly dark, put on dark sunglasses or goggles. Sensory deprivation.
Audio: David Bowie: 'Warszawa'.
Sign: Jesus dies upon the cross.

We are going into the darkest of our souls. We follow the Man on his journey into the bleakest of countries, the most desolate of places.

Put on the glasses. They place you in a space that is unremittingly dark.

Unforgivingly dismal.

But this is not as dark as it gets. Put your head into the box, where light is even further from your eyes.

Here you see what one ought not to see. Here the obscene becomes palpable, the unspoken said loud, the unthinkable made plain.

The Man dies.

Not immediately, oh no. A slow, painful and bleak death, where the life-force is drained out of the Man, until, in exhaustion, he gives up his spirit to God.

Wait.

Wait in the dark.

Sotto voce:
Our Father, who art in heaven,
hallowed be thy name;
thy kingdom come;
thy will be done,
on earth as it is in heaven.
Give us this day our daily bread.
And forgive us our trespasses,
as we forgive those who trespass against us.
And lead us not into temptation;
but deliver us from evil. Amen.

Glory be to the Father,
and to the Son,
and to the Holy Spirit.
As it was in the beginning,
is now, and ever shall be,
world without end. Amen.

(*Please return the goggles to the station. Thank you.*)

13. Taken Down

Station: video of the Pieta from The Passion of the Christ.
Audio: Philip Glass: 'Koyaanisqatsi'.
Sign: Jesus is placed in his Mother's arms.

Amid tears and wailing, the lifeless body is pulled down and unceremoniously dumped into the arms of his mourning Mother.

The soldiers get on with their work of removing the other corpses, disregarding the Man, now in their eyes no longer a man but a lump of lifeless nothing.

But to his mother, he remains something: something to be treated gently, and something to be treasured.

Do you have someone to treasure? You may not be related to them, you may have known them all your life, or for only a short time. They may have a huge impact on your life, or it may be the beginnings of a beautiful relationship; they may have borne you into this world; or walked with you through difficult times; no matter, what matters more is that they matter to you.

Think about them, recall for a moment special moments you shared with them: times of joy and laughter, times of intimacy, times of sadness and togetherness. Hold those moments as precious in your heart, turn them over like an exquisite piece of jewellery. These are special initmate relationships that should be treasured, stored away to be brought out when you feel sadness and loss at its most palpable.

Have you ever lost someone you loved deeply? Does that loss still pain you? The Man lay lifeless in his Mother's arms, and she wished to take away the pain, to fill the loss, to return to how it once was, to wipe away the tears and to restore the whole. She knows.

She grieves. Grieves with you.

Take him down, and care for him.

Sotto voce:
Hail Mary, full of grace, the Lord is with thee.
Blessed art thou among women, and blessed is the fruit of thy womb, Jesus.
Holy Mary, Mother of God,
pray for us sinners now, and at the hour of our death.

14. Entombed

Station: electric fridge, place hand inside to feel coolness.
Audio: Proost: 'Inward Journey' (Labyrinth instrumental).
Sign: Jesus is placed in the tomb.

Cold. Dark. Dank.

The lifeless corpse is placed in the tomb. A tomb hewn out of the solid rock, a tomb intended for someone else, but pressed into service by a friend.

Imagine how the disciples felt as they carried the bloodied body, rushing to get it stowed before sundown, before the day of enforced idleness began.

Put your hand into the coldness of this tomb. Feel the icy air upon you. Once they rolled the stone in place, the Man was trapped in here – a ton of rock over the entrance. This is a one-way ticket.

There can be no doubt the Man was dead. Water and blood flowed from his side when pierced, separated blood filling the lungs, which can only happen in death. Yes, the execution squad did their task well.

Feel the coolness of the tomb, sense the isolation and the darkness behind the rock. There is no escape from here.

Have you ever felt that you were in the pit of despair, the darkest place, the lowest hole? But you do not go to those remote and lonely places alone; if you ascend to the highest mountain or the depth of the ocean, God will be with you. There can be no escape from him.

They say that it is always darkest before the dawn. Here, in the cold, dark tomb we must wait in silence.

It is within the power of God to resolve all things. But we must not place our expectations or impatience on God. It will happen.

It will happen in God's good time. We must be patient. We must wait.

Feel the coolness of the tomb. Wait.

Our Father, who art in heaven,
hallowed be thy name;
thy kingdom come;
thy will be done,
on earth as it is in heaven.
Give us this day our daily bread.
And forgive us our trespasses,
as we forgive those who trespass against us.
And lead us not into temptation;
but deliver us from evil. Amen.

15. Resurrected

Station: step around the corner into a really bright light. See nothing. Emptiness.
Fans. AmbiPur scent or crushed herbs.
Audio: Castillos de Arena: 'Deep and Wide'.
Sign: Jesus is risen!

Come. Step into the marvellous light.

It is the unseen event, the hidden happening. We do not know how it happened, and can only imagine how it was.

But we have the evidence, we have the knowledge of the truth that it actually happened, that what was once cold and lifeless, bloodied and bruised, is now once again with us.

Not a ghost: for a ghost cannot eat, cannot breathe upon his closest friends and through this pass on that most precious essence of life, cannot fire the hearts of those who have seen beyond their doubts and fears and actually *dared* to believe. To take that step out, to ignore what the head suggests and to embrace what your senses tell you – that he is alive!

In this brilliant light, a light which illumes even the darkest of hearts, you may be able to find a solution to your fears; as you bask in the warm light of the risen one, you may be able to find comfort and peace, refreshment and joy. There is no place for the shadows of your fears in this space, no corner in which your anxieties may lurk, no place from which your insecurities may hide.

Come. Step into the light, open your heart and feel the warm breeze that embraces you. The unlikely has become real. The God for whom nothing is impossible has made it tangible.

There is hope. There is redemption. There is victory.

There is the Man.

Glory be to the Father,
and to the Son,
and to the Holy Spirit.
As it was in the beginning,

is now, and ever shall be,
world without end. Amen.

Conclusion

Audio: Massive Attack: 'Teardrop'.
Sign: The end ... or the beginning?

Your Via Dolorosa has come to an end, but your journey has not.

You will travel away from this place and back into the world. A world that has only the slightest idea about what you have just experienced.

This Way of Sorrows may have bounced off you, bored you rigid or just have been a mild diversion for a few minutes.

This Way of Truth may have made you stop and think about your own walk of faith, of your own journey with God and his part in your life.

This Way of Life may have touched your inner soul, and opened up for you new possibilities of worship and engagement with the sacred, the divine, to begin to perceive the unknowable and to know the imperceptible.

You may have found this journey to be none of these things; but we travel on with our life's pilgrimage, we move on to an unknown destination, to God knows where.

God indeed knows where, for he walks beside you, he is your travelling companion and your destination.

Go now: go in faith, go in peace, go to love and serve the Lord and to do his will. Touch others with the grace that has touched you and see the face of the risen Lord in each and every one you encounter on this life's journey. And the Blessing of God Almighty, +Father, Son and Holy Spirit, be upon you and remain with you, this day and always. Amen.

Return your headset to the beginning, and thank you.

4.6.2 Stations of the Spirit

Based on Galatians 5.22–23: 'But the fruit of the Spirit is love, joy, peace, patience, kindness, goodness, faithfulness, gentleness, self-control; against such things there is no law.'

The Stations are arranged around the site, perhaps in small tents. The audio first takes you to the Station and then asks you perform the activity described in each, so there are ten tracks in all. Each tent has laminates indicating the track to be played and quotes, scriptures and reflections to assist each prayer station.[14]

Required Items:

- Four one-person tents.
- 128Mb MP3 players.
- Various direction signs.
- Signing-out book.
- Comments and feedback book.
- A number of balti dishes to hold things.
- Bag of large palm-sized stones.
- Sponges/Body Shop lilies.
- Large water bucket.
- Red ribbons, cut into 6–8 inch strips.
- Felt-tip pens.
- Large crucifix or similar.
- Quantity of fake fur.
- Silk lilies or, even better, a daily supply of fresh lilies.
- Hand cream.
- Pillows, duvets.

1: Introduction

Audio: Massive Attack: 'Teardrop'.

Come …

Come, walk with us.

Come, step outside your busy lives, step outside everything that's on your mind, your friends and your exams, your families, your job. Whatever you're worried about, whatever stresses you out: leave it behind and come on a

---

14　These could be added at a later stage.

journey with the One who is always there to walk with you, the One who never gives up on you, no matter how difficult things get.

In one of his letters (to the Galatians; these days you'd find them in modern Turkey), St Paul tries to get people to see the difference Jesus can make in our lives. Paul sees that people who spend time with God are changed for ever by the experience. Just as a tree needs sunlight and water to go on growing and giving its fruit, we also need the presence of God's Spirit if we are to live life to the full as God desires. Paul speaks about a person bearing the fruits of the Spirit, and he makes a list of nine of them: love, joy, peace, patience, kindness, goodness, faithfulness, gentleness, self-control.

So, as we walk this journey of life, we pray for God's gift to us of all these fruits, all these gifts; we think about love and self-control, joy and peace, patience, gentleness, faithfulness, kindness and goodness. And because travelling is as much a part of the journey as the destination, each of these four tents of meeting-with-God has a reflection for the journey between each tent, as well as words and activities for you to do when you get there.

So savour the experience: let the word of God dwell deeply within you and concentrate on these tracks, for this journey is between you and God.

2: Love and Self-Control – Destination

Audio: Nirvana: 'Smells Like Teen Spirit'.

Love is all around.
All you need is love
Love is the drug.
Endless love.

Love, it would seem, is a major concern of our lives. Music and adverts are full of it. It fills our iPods and clogs up our TVs. We can't seem to get away from it. But what is this thing called love?

Eskimos have hundreds of words for snow: they see there's a difference between the light flakes that dance in the morning sunshine and the heavy, impenetrable drift.

In the same way, there are different ways to think about love. Of course, the songs we hear are mainly about the love between lovers, the 'I-love-you-baby-let's-get-together-and-make-lurve' type of love.

But there's also the love between a parent and a child, so you'd say, 'I love my mum or dad.'

Then there's the love between friends, or between brothers and sisters; and there's the selfless love we try to show one another as Christians, that love for our neighbour which Jesus talks about: it doesn't have a price-tag.

But It's all love. It's not all the same. It expresses the depth and wideness and beauty of all those things we know of as love; and still it fails to capture the love of God poured out for us.

God loves you as a parent loves a child – as one of his own.
He loves you with passion, with intimacy, closer than a lover.
God loves and celebrates you as you are – as a friend and a brother.
God loves you, regardless of whether you love him back. God's love has no strings attached, no conditions.

That's the most challenging thing about this sort of love, the love which Jesus pours out for us on the cross: it's not something we asked for, but still God gives it. God wasn't required to give it, he didn't have to; but he gives his love anyway, his amazing grace; it flows as freely as running water, and all we need to do is jump in and learn to swim in it.

3: Love and Self-Control – Station

Equipment: stones and sponges. Large bucket of water.
Audio: Proost: 'Inner Journey' (Labyrinth Instrumental).

Come into this Station. Enter and relax.

Love can be as soft as sponges, or feel as hard as stones. It can make us feel warm and enriched. It can frustrate us, especially when love is painful, when love is unreturned, or when the love someone has for us prevents us from following our own selfish desires: the parent who won't let us out all night is the one who loves us.

Pick up a stone. Cradle it in the palm of your hand. Feel its smoothness and its broken edges.

Examine it closely. It's been shaped by centuries of waves and weather, damaged by explosion, by digging and building. Yet here it is, in your hand, in this field. In this place. In your possession.

It has been shaped by experience, good and bad; just as we are shaped by our experiences of life, of love.

'I will take your heart of stone,' the prophet told the words of God to the people, 'and give you back a heart of flesh.'

Our experiences can make our hearts as cold as this stone, as tough as rock. Emotions can bounce off it and nothing can touch it.

Do we think this makes us strong? Do we think that by putting up a strong shield against people we'll save ourselves from being hurt?

Do you really want a heart of stone?

'I will take your heart of stone, and give you back a heart of flesh.'

As you cradle this stone in your hand, pass on to it all those feelings of hardness in your life: those times when you have rejected others, been indifferent to their needs, their suffering. Let your selfishness coat this stone.

Now gently drop it into the water, and let it sink. It takes away with it those feelings, its toughness absorbs the tough things in your life, and the stream of living water which Jesus speaks of washes those feelings away.

'I will take your heart of stone, and give you back a heart of flesh.'

A heart of flesh is a heart which beats to the rhythm of the world, a heart of flesh is one which is open to the needs of those it meets. A vulnerable heart is one that is open to the love of God.

Take up a sponge. It is soft and yielding, it is flexible, pliable, responsive. It moves with you, and it moves with life. It is a heart which is open for God.

'I will take your heart of stone, and give you back a heart of flesh.'

4: Joy and Peace – Destination

Audio: Prince: 'Sign of the Times'.

God has been known to do some dramatic things in the past: to level mountains and part waters, to bring dry bones back to life and to sort out this rabble of humanity by sending his only Son to sort us out.

But we can't always expect God to do the dramatic thing, put on a show especially for us, to give us proof beyond all doubt that he is indeed behind it all. It needs a bit of faith from us.

'Do not put the Lord your God to the test.'

We can't expect a lightshow especially for us, a hand reaching out from the clouds, pointing out our way

When Elijah went out to meet with God, he experienced all manner of loud and impressive things: winds, earthquakes, fires raging past him. But, we were told, God was not, was not in any of these signs of raw natural power. After the wind, the earth-shaking, the fire, came a still, small voice, a breath like a sigh. And God was in that distant sigh.

As we travel to our next Station to experience the joy and the peace of God, think of what gives you joy. Events. Places. People. Activities. What makes you happy?

What do you do to fill others with joy? A visit? A smile? Going out of your way to make a difference to the life of someone?

5: Love and Peace – Station

Equipment: strips of ribbon and pens. A large crucifix with perhaps a balti dish to place the ribbons in.
Audio: Moonwater: 'Sofa Loafer'.

We have so much to be thankful for. Our lives, our friends, those whom we love, and the simple reality of being alive itself is enough to be thankful for.

Take one of these ribbons and think of the joys in your lives. Write one or two of them on the ribbon and place it here: a shrine of prayer to God, a place of peace where the joy of God can reach through and touch you through your prayers and thanksgivings.

After you have written these things, hold them up to God in thanksgiving. Thinking of the good things that God brings about in your life, you may feel a sense of peace.

There isn't enough peace in the world; there isn't enough calm.

Sometimes we fill our lives up with chatter, with twitter, with texts and instant messages: so much communication that we lose connection with the One who is always there to listen and be there for us.

In order to plug in to God, in order to hear what he is saying to us, in order to make the connection, we need to unplug from the rest of it. There is a rhythm in your life which does not come through your ears. There is a beat which only you can sense. Listen.

Audio cuts out.

It is there. Can you feel your heartbeat? Put your hand on the left side of your chest. Can you feel it? It is the rhythm of your life. Listen. Feel.

God speaks to you like a still, small voice crying out in the distance. He calls you. Listen. Feel.

Audio fades in.

We don't always get enough time to stop and listen to the dancebeat which is inside of us all the time: a rhythm which moves us through the dance of life. Other things might block out or hide it, but that doesn't mean that it isn't there. Take the opportunity to experience that deep peace – give thanks to God and be blessed with that peace.

6: Patience, Faithfulness and Gentleness – Destination

Audio: Take That: 'Patience' loop.

Good things will come your way.

All you need is the faith to carry on this journey.

There are times when the journey will be hard. There will be distractions, there will be frustrations. There will times when you want give up and give in.

The journey of your life is a journey towards God. It is a journey which you do not travel alone, for it is a path which has been trodden for centuries by the wise and the foolish, the rich and the poor, the sorted and the messed up.

God calls everyone home.

Never lose sight of the destination, and travel there with faith.

7: Patience, Faithfulness and Gentleness – Station

Equipment: fake fur, silk flowers, fresh flowers would be even better, but they'd need to be replaced each day.
Audio: Nitin Sawhney: 'Spark' from Philtre *(instrumental).*

We want it, and we want it now. We want it yesterday. We want it in full and we'd rather not pay the full price of it.

Unfortunately, life is not always like eBay. Things take time. Things that are truly worth it are things that are worth taking time over – like a carefully carved statue, a work of art, they all take time, take effort, and require patience.

The lilies of the field, Jesus said, don't get stressed out with work, they don't break their backs to earn money just to stay in fashion, and yet they look just fine. Take some time to examine these flowers at this Station, twirl them in your hands and look at the beauty which is held in each. No supermodel can match this, no fashion writer can encapsulate this fully. No movie star is the equal of this lily, and no surgery, no airbrush, no Photoshop is needed.

You, too, are one of God's creations, you are as lovely as this. You are as unique, and special to God. If he looks after the birds of the air, don't you know that he will look after you?

Be comforted in that – experience his gentle love. Run your fingers through the fur: don't worry, it's not real, but it feels good, doesn't it? It can be soothing and comforting, and perhaps you might even get a sense of warmth and proximity in it: relax, be comforted, experience luxury, have a sense of security. You are loved and protected by the God who knows every hair on your heads, knew you before you were formed in the womb, knows you by name.

It's so easy to miss the hand of God in your life: think about those times when things go wrong, and recall how often you blame him for your own bad choices.

Think about those times when things have gone well, and you congratulate yourself for your skill and artistry, and forget God's hand in it.

Have faith. Be assured. Know God.

Pray, hope and don't worry.

God cares for you. You more than anything else in all creation. You are special. You are loved.

8: Kindness and Goodness – Destination

Audio: David Bowie: 'All Saints'.

We are always being told about how we have to be good.

'You're a good boy/a good girl.'

From our earliest ages, it was our goodness which was always being judged, by parents, maiden aunts and people in the supermarket.

Goodness is a virtue which is therefore quite underestimated. What does it mean to be good?

At school they often talked about 'Gentle Jesus, meek and mild' as though he spent his whole time swanning around Judea with his head in the clouds and being nice to the animals.

Was this the same man who caused such scandal with the authorities and those who knew better because he reached out to the poor, to the marginalized, to those different and difficult?

Was this the man who got so outraged at the way they treated God's house like a supermarket that he kicked them all out with his bare hands?

Was this the man who lived rough, moving from place to place preaching the good news without a home or knowing where the next meal was coming from, but trusting in the Father to meet his needs?

Was this the man who was tough enough to survive beating, whipping and being dragged through the streets before completing his most important, toughest work of all on the cross?

What's meek and mild about that?

Jesus shows us a goodness which flows out from being filled with the love of God, not from conforming to the expectations of others, a goodness which enables him to live for God, in God's way, not moulded by the constraints of polite society or authority figures.

This radical goodness might call you to reach out to those who Christ reached out to: the poor, those on the edge of society, the lonely, those in your midst that 'proper' society ignores, the sort who others think aren't worthy of kindness, the ones who Christ met with, and changed.

Be good. Be strong. Be prepared to be different.

Be like Christ.

9: Kindness and Goodness – Station

Equipment: duvets, cushions, hand cream.
Audio: Windows installation track.

Come in and relax in here. You have made a long journey so far, and you must be weary. Sit down among these cushions and make yourself at home. God is here.

It's a chance to pamper yourself a little. There's some hand cream here. Take a little. Before you rub it in, have a smell. Breathe in deeply. Every kindness in this world is a gift from God. Every kindness you show to others is a gift of God through you. You are God's agent in this world: when you follow his lead, do his work, share his love, you are the hands of God.

This bloke was going through a rough part of town. It wasn't his town, and he didn't really belong here. You can think of your own local tensions:

football teams, chav and grunge, colour of skin, there's no end of examples. Whatever it was, he was out on his own, in a vulnerable place, in the wrong place.

He was set upon, beaten, robbed and left in a bleeding, bruised pile on the pavement.

As our victim was lying there, he thought he could see someone coming down the street dressed in a dog collar – the local priest. He was saved! But the local priest had so much on his mind, Masses to say and masses to do and he just looked past the man on the ground – a head so far in the clouds that he couldn't see the need in front of him.

A little while later, our victim lying there with bruised and swollen eyes thought he could see one of his own – the same football shirt, the same dress code, the same hairstyle or cap or whatever we choose to show our individuality with by being just like all our mates – he was saved! But his brother in fashion didn't want to get blood on him, didn't want to get involved, didn't want to put aside his plans for the day and deal with it – his life was already far too full to bother with this need.

When the victim thought that was it, that the end was near, there came another standing over him. Different. Different colour football shirt, different style of music coming over the iPod. Different. This means trouble, this means the end.

But the stranger, the man who had no ties to our victim, was the one to help him up, to get him to the hospital, to sort out the paperwork and the police, to help the victim get his life back together. He went out of his own way to make a difference to the victim, went the extra mile. Saw out what was right.

'Which of these three', asked Jesus, 'was like a neighbour?'

The one who showed him kindness, they answered. Not the one whom everyone expects to be holy. Not the one who seemed to be from the same family, the same mindset, the same tribe. The one who looked beyond the badges and the labels and saw the need of another human being.

Jesus then gave those to whom he told this story a simple command:

'Go then, and do likewise.'

Goodness does not necessarily mean holiness. You can try and be so religious, so caught up in the ways of doing church that you miss what the point is. You can be looking so hard for God on the inside that you forget that sometimes God needs you to share that gift with others.

All of these fruits of the Spirit make a wonderful difference deep in your own life, but if you keep them there they will make no difference in this world. These gifts are gifts to be given out through you to others. All others. All kinds. All ways. All perspectives. All are part of God's wonderful creation and all are worthy of God's grace, his kindness and his goodness, through you.

You can make a difference. You are anointed with this scent of heaven, blessed with his riches. You receive God's goodness and kindness.

And so as he said:

'Go then, and do likewise.'

10: Return

Audio: Massive Attack: 'Teardrop'.

We have travelled and we have explored. We have journeyed and sought out the fruits of the Spirit of God.

God gives us these fruits, but not just to keep to ourselves. They can only be truly fruitful when they are shared with others. As you return from this journey and re-enter the real world, you have the opportunity to share your fruits with others – to share your love, to demonstrate your self-control, to bring joy to all, to make peace where there is disquiet; to show patience, be gentle and be a beacon of faith; to be kind and good, and daily demonstrate Christ within you shining out towards others.

By these fruits will they see Jesus in you.

St Teresa of Avila told us:

Christ has no body on earth but yours,
no hands but yours, no feet but yours.
Yours are the eyes through which Christ's compassion

for the world is to look out;
yours are the feet with which he is to go about doing good;
and yours are the hands with which he is to bless us now.

Travel back to where we started out together.

Go forth from this place and share those fruits with others.
May you be filled with joy and peace, patience, gentleness, love and kindness,
and may the blessing of God Almighty: +Father, Son and Holy Spirit, be upon
you and remain with you, this day and always.

Amen.

4.7 Rituals and Meditations

This section effectively captures everything else which cannot conveniently be labelled.

4.7.1 Names of God

This is an alphabetical list of some of the many names and titles of Father, Son and Spirit in scripture. At Walsingham we used these names one after the other, culminating in 'Word', which as the festival was focusing on scripture, was the most appropriate. You might like to manipulate these in other ways, perhaps more slowly and meditatively; or perhaps by illustration.

Advocate: 1 John 2.1.

Almighty: Revelation 1.8.

Alpha: Revelation 1.8.

Amen: Revelation 3.14.

Angel of the Lord: Genesis 16.7.

Anointed One: Psalm 2.2.

Apostle: Hebrews 3.1.

Author and Perfecter of our Faith:
    Hebrews 12.2.

Beginning: Revelation 21.6.

Bishop of Souls: 1 Peter 2.25.

Branch: Zechariah 3.8.

Bread of Life: John 6.35,48.

Bridegroom: Matthew 9.15.

Carpenter: Mark 6.3.

Chief Shepherd: 1 Peter 5.4.

The Christ: Matthew 1.16.

Comforter: Jeremiah 8.18.

Consolation of Israel: Luke 2.25.

Cornerstone: Ephesians 2.20.

Dayspring: Luke 1.78.

Day Star: 2 Peter 1.19.

Deliverer: Romans 11.26.

Desire of Nations: Haggai 2.7.

Emmanuel: Matthew 1.23.

End: Revelation 21.6.

Everlasting Father: Isaiah 9.6.

First Fruits: 1 Corinthians 15.23.

Foundation: Isaiah 28.16.

Fountain: Zechariah 13.1.

Friend of Sinners: Matthew 11.19.

Gate for the Sheep: John 10.7.

Gift of God: 2 Corinthians 9.15.

Glory of God: Isaiah 60.1.

God: John 1.1.

Good Shepherd: John 10.11.

Governor: Matthew 2.6.

Great Shepherd: Hebrews 13.20.

Guide: Psalm 48.14.

Head of the Church: Colossians 1.18.

High Priest: Hebrews 3.1.

Holy One of Israel: Isaiah 41.14.

Horn of Salvation: Luke 1.69.

I Am: Exodus 3.14.

Jehovah: Psalm 83.18.

Jesus: Matthew 1.21.

King of Israel: Matthew 27.42.

King of Kings: 1 Timothy 6.15;
   Revelation 19.16.

Lamb of God: John 1.29.

Last Adam: 1 Corinthians 15.45.

Life: John 11.25.

Light of the World: John 8.12; John
   9.5.

Lion of the Tribe of Judah: Revelation
   5.5.

Lord of Lords: 1 Timothy 6.15;
   Revelation 19.16.

Master: Matthew 23.8.

Mediator: 1 Timothy 2.5.

Messiah: John 1.41.

Mighty God: Isaiah 9.6.

Morning Star: Revelation 22.16.

Nazarene: Matthew 2.23.

Omega: Revelation 1.8.

Passover Lamb: 1 Corinthians 5.7.

Physician: Matthew 9.12.

Potentate: 1 Timothy 6.15.

Priest: Hebrews 4.15.

Prince of Peace: Isaiah 9.6.

Prophet: Acts 3.22.

Propitiation: 1 John 2.2.

Purifier: Malachi 3.3.

Rabbi: John 1.49.

Ransom: 1 Timothy 2.6.

Redeemer: Isaiah 41.14.

Refiner: Malachi 3.2.

Refuge: Isaiah 25.4.

Resurrection: John 11.25.

Righteousness: Jeremiah 23.6.

Rock: Deuteronomy 32.4.

Root of David: Revelation 22.16.

Rose of Sharon: Song of Solomon 2.1.

Ruler of God's Creation: Revelation
   3.14.

Sacrifice: Ephesians 5.2.

Saviour: 2 Samuel 22.47; Luke 1.47.

Second Adam: 1 Corinthians 15.47.

Seed of Abraham: Galatians 3.16.

Seed of David: 2 Timothy 2.8.

Seed of the Woman: Genesis 3.15.

Servant: Isaiah 42.1.

Shepherd: 1 Peter 2.25.

Shiloh: Genesis 49.10.

Son of David: Matthew 15.22.

Son of God: Luke 1.35.

Son of Man: Matthew 18.11.

Son of Mary: Mark 6.3.

Son of the Most High: Luke 1.32.

Stone: Isaiah 28.16.

Sun of Righteousness: Malachi 4.2.

Teacher: Matthew 26.18.

Truth: John 14.6.

Way: John 14.6.

Wonderful Counsellor: Isaiah 9.6.

Word: John 1.1.

Vine: John 15.1.

4.7.2 Nuts: A Meditation Based on the Revelations of Mother Julian of Norwich

And in this he showed me a little thing, the quantity of a hazelnut, lying in the palm of my hand, as it seemed. And it was as round as any ball. I looked upon it with the eye of my understanding, and thought, 'What may this be?' And it was answered generally thus, 'It is all that is made.' I marvelled how it might last, for I thought it might suddenly have fallen to nought for littleness. And I was answered in my understanding: it lasts and ever shall, for God loves it. And so have all things their beginning by the love of God.

Take a hazelnut.

Imagine, you hold the whole universe in your hand, all its galaxies, planetary systems, stars, planets – wonder at its size – God made it, God loves it, God keeps it.

Imagine, you hold the earth in your hand, all its countries and oceans, its flora and fauna, its weather systems and currents, its cities and villages, its cultures and communities – wonder at its complexity – God made it, God loves it, God keeps it.

Imagine, you hold this community in your hand, its people, their families, their personalities, their stories, their joys and their sorrows, their gifts – wonder at its diversity – God made us, God loves us, God keeps us.

Imagine, you hold yourself in your hand, your story, your strengths and weaknesses, your dreams and your fears, your struggles and celebrations, your spirit – wonder at your beauty – God made you, God loves you, God keeps you.

In this little thing I saw three properties. The first is that God made it. The second that he loves it. And the third, that God keeps it. But what is this to me? Truly, the Creator, the Keeper, the Lover. For until I am substantially oned to him, I may never have full rest nor true bliss. That is to say, until I be so fastened to him that there is nothing that is made between my God and me.

God made it, God loves it, God keeps it.
God made you, God loves you, God keeps you.
God made us, God loves us, God keeps us.

He who was before the beginning,
he who is one with the whole,
he who was not created but was,
he through whom everything was made,
he who came to walk among us,
he who was born into poverty,
he who had all power at his disposal,
he who gave it away for the least of us,
he who wore the mockers' crown,
he who was stripped,
he who was whipped,
he who bled for us,
he who shed for us,
he who cried for us,
he who died for us,
he who lived again,
he who lives with us now and for ever.

God, for your goodness, give me yourself, for you are all that I
    need.
May I never ask anything that is less than you,
for if I ask anything that is less, I know I will never be satisfied,
only in you have I all that I need.
Your goodness encompasses all of creation and all of your works,
your goodness goes beyond all that we can see,
your goodness is endless, for you are endless.
You created us for yourself,
and re-created us through your Passion, your love and sacrifice.
Keep us in your deepest love and wrap us in your total goodness.
As we rest in you,
all shall be well,
and all shall be well,
and all manner of things shall be well.

4.7.3 Thirst

It's been a hot day.
You've been out in the heat,
had nothing to drink,
And are thirsty.

'My soul thirsts for you, my body longs for you, in a dry and weary land where there is no water.'

What does it feel like to be thirsty?
Your mouth is dry,
you are weary,
your whole body longs for water.

'Come, all you who are thirsty, come to the waters.'

Jesus feels like this travelling through Samaria on a hot day. Tired from the journey, he sits down by the well. A Samaritan woman comes to draw water. Jesus asks her for a drink.

'Will you give me a drink?'

Samaritans are distrusted by Jews.
Women are not to be approached in public:
she is surprised and asked why Jesus does this.
He replies:

'If you knew the gift of God and who it is that asks you for a drink, you would have asked him and he would have given you living water.'

Living water?
What's that?
How will Jesus get it without a bucket?

'Everyone who drinks this water (from the well) will be thirsty again, but whoever drinks the water I give will never thirst. Indeed, the water I give will become in them a spring of water welling up to eternal life.'

Never be thirsty again …
A spring of water welling up to eternal life.
The woman asks for some of this water.
Think about your own thirst;
imagine being with Jesus at the well as he speaks of this life-giving water;
it's freely available to all who are thirsty.

'If anyone is thirsty let them come to me and drink . . .'

Speak to Jesus
if you want to ask him for this water.

Slide: take some time to pray and ask God to quench your thirst. Run your hands into the living water. You are washed clean.

Let this drink be the gift of God's life-giving Spirit. As you drink, be refreshed.

4.7.4 Renewal of Baptismal Promises

Each Easter, we remind ourselves of our hope in Christ by renewing the promises we made, or which were made for us in Baptism.

Baptism is a sacramental sign of God's saving work in us, using an outward symbol to express an inward act of God's grace, a gift so wonderful that words themselves are inadequate and we have to shut up for once; turn to ritual; turn to symbol.

As each day we are called to pick up our cross and follow Christ, each day we try to live out our baptismal promises.

In baptism, God calls us out of darkness into his marvellous light.
To follow Christ means dying to sin and rising to new life with him.
Therefore I ask you all:

Do you reject the devil and all rebellion against God?
We reject them.

Do you renounce the deceit and corruption of evil?
We renounce them.

Do you repent of the sins that separate us from God and neighbour?
We repent of them.

Do you turn to Christ as Saviour?
We turn to Christ.

You are encouraged to come forward again to this stream of living water, dip into it and make the sign of the cross on your body or your forehead, to remind yourself that you are washed clean by the Holy Spirit through your Baptism, both then, now and for evermore.

The sign of the cross is the sign of victory over sin and death. Do not be ashamed to confess the faith of Christ crucified.

**Fight valiantly as a disciple of Christ
against sin, the world and the devil,
and remain faithful to Christ to the end of your life.**

4.7.5 Ashing

Nowhere are the physical and the spiritual more closely bound together than in the rituals of Ash Wednesday. 'Remember you are dust and to dust you shall return' is a visceral reminder of our fallenness, but more importantly, of God's grace.

The smudge of ash
on a white brow.
Darkness and light.
Repent and turn to Christ.
Darkness and light,
ash mixed with oil.
Oil to anoint,
oil to heal.
Last year's negatives,
(the darkness)
burned

and taken up as a cross
with confidence
into the light.

(Ruth Innes)[15]

One of the most powerful penitential rites was for Palm Sunday. We invited the congregation to write their confessions on palm crosses and then burnt them with a blow-torch in a big bowl. Just remember to put something underneath what will become a very hot bowl, and to take them out immediately after the Absolution, as burnt palm crosses are very cloying!

4.8 Affirmations of Faith

The Creeds are accepted statements of faith derived from the Ecumenical Councils. They are inviolate. However, it is perfectly acceptable to draw from them and through them affirmations of faith. These may be simplified or expanded.

4.8.1 God Waits

God waits for us,
not like a lion ready to pounce
if we let our guard down,
not like an interfering in-law
but like an old friend who's seen it all before
and likes us anyway,
with whom we can spend time
without having to pretend or explain.

Read aloud by all:

**We believe in God,
three in one,
Father, Son, Spirit,
paradox,**

---

15 With permission of the author.

mystery,
elemental.

We believe in a God of justice,
compassion, mercy, hope.
And first, a God of love,
love personified,
incarnated.

We believe in God,
The Mother of creation.
God, the father of humanity.
God, the lover of us all.

We believe we are called:
to activity out of passivity and apathy,
by the Son of God,
through his actions,
calling down through history,
borne on the wings of the Spirit.

We believe we are called:
to community with each other,
through Christ, the thread
weaving us all together.

We believe that God has no favourites,
pulls no punches,
leaves no stone unturned.
We believe that life is hard,
we believe that life is beautiful.
So, we believe, does God.

4.8.2 Community Affirmation

We took a text of an affirmation of faith and recorded it with a wide variety of members of the faith community: young, old, individuals, small and large groups. By cutting them together it provided a wonderful collage of a community of faith. This works better with simpler texts such as this *Common Worship* text drawn from Ephesians 3.

We believe in God the Father,
from whom every family
in heaven and on earth is named.

We believe in God the Son,
who lives in our hearts through faith,
and fills us with his love.

We believe in God the Holy Spirit,
who strengthens us
with power from on high.

We believe in one God:
Father, Son and Holy Spirit.
Amen.

4.9 Blessing

4.9.1 Act of Commitment

We are pilgrims on a common journey with Christ as our guide.
Will you be faithful and determined in discipleship?
With the help of God, we will.

We have gathered around the table and been fed for the road.
Will you share the good news of Christ with those whom you meet?
With the help of God, we will.

The Spirit breathes many gifts to build up the body.
Will you use your gifts in the service of others?
With the help of God, we will.

The path we travel brings pain and sadness, joy and delight.
Will you endure on this way to bring in the Kingdom?
With the help of God, we will.

May the boldness of the Spirit transform you.
May the gentleness of the Spirit lead you.
May the gifts of the Spirit equip you
to proclaim afresh in this generation the unchanging love of Christ.

And the blessing of God: +Father, Son and Holy Spirit,
be upon you and remain with you, this morning, this day and always.

Amen.

(Mark Steadman)[16]

16 With permission of the author.